THE SEAGULLS BEST EVER SEASON

The incredible story of Brighton's 2022-23 season

TONY NOBLE

FOREWORD BY JOHNNY CANTOR

First Edition.
First published 2023

Published by:
Morgan Lawrence Publishing Services Limited
Ridge House Annexe
16 Main Ridge West
Boston
Lincolnshire
PE21 6QQ
www.morganlawrence.co.uk
email: info@morganlawrence.co.uk
Company number: 12910264

©Tony Noble, 2023
ISBN: 9781739296926

Edited by Scott McCarthy

A CIP catalogue record is available for this book from the
British Library.

Photographs are courtesy of:
Rachel Thompson, Johnny Cantor, Tony Noble, Luke Nicoli,
and Brighton and Hove Albion/Paul Hazlewood.

Cover design by LCgrapix. Cover photos by Brighton and Hove
Albion/Paul Hazlewood and Rachel Thompson.

Every effort has been made to trace the copyright. Any oversight
will be rectified in future editions at the earliest opportunity.

Printed and bound in Bulgaria
by Pulsio Print.

Contents

Sponsored by

PREFACE

I WAS BORN at Southlands Hospital in Shoreham by Sea in Sussex in September 1955 and have my very first memories of Brighton & Hove Albion of course at the Goldstone Ground on Old Shoreham Road. I was lucky enough and it was safe enough in those days that my mum would say to me, "Here is the money to go to watch Brighton" and I would catch the number 5 bus from Hangleton near the Grenadier pub and scramble down to the front of the North Stand by the wall and wave my rattle furiously. What great fun times they were.

So, it was a shock to a young lad who was told by his parents that we all had to move away because of my dad's job. That was after the World Cup of 1966, and while I was at Hangleton Junior School with Mr Phillips as our football teacher we went on to win a football medal for the local school team. On our school side was Richard Jennings, the son of Albion player Roy Jennings. What fond memories I have of that period. It was the only football medal I would ever win. Yes, I still have it!

I never was able to go back to watch the Albion for many reasons, until I semi-retired quite recently. It was in the last months of Chris Hughton's time as manager of the club, that I had my first taste of the Amex Stadium and how wonderful and proud I felt that the club could fight back as they had from near extinction.

Following the club closely having elderly parents in a sheltered accommodation, which was just a stone's throw from the Withdean Stadium, meant that in later life I heard many a roar from there and so wished I could play a part. However, my time came around and now I really relish the chance to visit the stadium at Falmer on home matches.

I find it difficult to visit the away games and so I am always there listening to Johnny Cantor and Warren Aspinall as this book will show. I responded to a message in early 2021 from Scott McCarthy at We Are Brighton.Com who was looking to recruit people to write for the website. I was accepted and that began the series of articles for the 2021-2022 season, 'Thoughts of a 66-year-old first-time season ticket holder'.

The reason for putting these articles together and producing the first self-published little book was to tick a box and fulfil another boyhood dream of mine — becoming a journalist/writer. I wanted to work as a journalist while at school, however, you must pass your exams if you all recall. Well, I failed the lot! All nine O levels and it was not until much later in life that exams and tests became easier for me. By that time I was serving as a firefighter for Kent Fire Rescue and latterly as a Police Officer for Surrey Police as a Detective. I was in fact the first Cybercrime Detective for Surrey Police back in the early 2000s.

Now of course as the lads of all done so amazingly well under our coach Roberto De Zerbi, a second book has to be done. As some of you may recall, the book is set up, so you can follow the season from start to finish like a diary and all the matches tell of the ups and downs of not just the games themselves but the story behind each one and how I coped keeping up. I hope you enjoy the read this was an amazing year from a supporter's eye view!

The 2023-2024 season will be so exciting too. We wish our team and coaches well as they embark on making more club history for Brighton & Hove Albion F. C. Thank you for all the enjoyment, we get from supporting such a great team who are now becoming known in all corners of the globe.

Up The Albion!

Tony Noble
August 2023

FOREWORD
By Johnny Cantor

THEY SAY FOOTBALL never stops. It's true, it has a never-ending cycle and that is part of what makes us love it so much. However, sometimes it is best to stop, reflect, re-live, and savour those special moments.

Ever since I began covering Brighton and Hove Albion for the BBC, the club has been on an upward trajectory. In the 2022-2023 season, the Seagulls broke more records with a highest-ever finish and an unprecedented step towards European football. Tony's book charts an incredible season in which the club overcame huge disruption to achieve another of Tony's (Bloom) dreams. People come and go in football. This season Graham Potter and his staff left the Amex and Roberto de Zerbi entered the spotlight.

As supporters plan for trips to the continent it is easy to forget some of the fantastic games and wonderful goals. The historic win at Old Trafford seems a long time ago but started a campaign that exceeded the expectations of even the most optimistic of fans.

The difficulty in choosing a player of the season shows just how good the players were. I can't examine them all here but each one played their part. Meanwhile the manager not only developed the players he also introduced a style that heralded plaudits from across the globe, including a certain Pep Guardiola.

It is very difficult to distil the last 10 months into a few magical moments but no one who was there will forget Enciso's two wonder goals, the latter against Manchester City earning *Match of the Day*'s goal of the season award. The penalty taken by Alexis Mac Allister as the clock ticked late on at the Amex was also incredible to witness. Some of the team goals also deserve to be remembered as that was what this season was all about — teamwork. The trip to the Emirates was something special.

Of course, not everything is plain sailing when it comes to football. The agony of the penalty shootout at Wembley was hard to take but I think Albion fans rightly recognise that Solly March deserves support for his huge contribution, particularly in the first half of the season and not criticism for one miss of the target. You win as a team, and you lose as a team. The emergence of March, the recall to the England squad for Lewis Dunk, and the Premier League debut of Jack Hinselwood are all aspects that the club and its fanbase can be proud of. Local boys doing well at their local club.

What next? Well, a European adventure. Perhaps the only missing piece of the puzzle is silverware, but that may not be far away. For now, though, it's important to say 'thanks for the memories' this year. There were joyous times both at the Amex and across the country, and I will never forget my times on the microphone describing the action. I hope this book serves as a way for you to re-live them once again.

Johnny Cantor
BBC Radio Sussex
Presenter

SPONSOR'S MESSAGE
Seagull Travel

SEAGULL TRAVEL IS proud to be the Brighton and Hove Albion Football Club 'Official Fans Travel Supplier' since the Amex opened and even before that, running coaches to the Play-Off Final at Cardiff in 2004.

We are run by lifelong BHAFC fans who appreciate the ups and the downs of being a supporter but with Europe to plan for, 2023 is looking like a wonderful year.

The Seagull Travel network of buses and coaches from over 200 pick-up locations in Sussex, Hampshire, Surrey, and Kent was pitched to many fans from a temporary cabin at the Amex whilst the Stadium was being constructed — the rest is history!

Our extensive network serves areas well where there is no other suitable travel option but we also see high demand from areas close to the Amex due to our professional and reliable service, which includes coach parking at the Amex which is only 200 yards from the East Stand entrance gates.

Our service is pre-booked and offers two product options: fans can buy one travel season ticket for all 19 home Premier League matches, and subject to availability, fans can buy match-by-match seats.

Also, excitedly we will be launching soon our first ever Home Europa League travel pass to include the guaranteed three home group stage matches.

At this stage, we are planning to run coaches to European away matches where distance allows.

Bookings are primarily made online via www.seagull-travel.co.uk or by calling 01903 232155.

Darren Gallis
Director
Event Travel Hub

SeagullTravel
Official Fans Travel Supplier

Sponsor

CHAPTER 1
August 2022

Team v Individuals: Brighton showed Man United the value of togetherness.

THE SUMMER BREAK seems to have flown by with so much happening, from player sales to the Women's Euros. It only feels like yesterday that Brighton beat West Ham in the final game of the 2021-22 season and here we were, another much-awaited new Premier League season getting underway on Friday evening.

Arsenal away at Crystal Palace kicked us off. Having watched on television as Arsenal won 2-0, I felt the football was nowhere near as good as what we had seen from the Albion in the last few matches at the end of last season. Little did I know that Brighton would be even better in their opener away at Manchester United on Sunday.

Before we talk about Old Trafford, there is one other thing I want to tackle – the Brighton Fans' Forum, held on Thursday 4th August in the Mayo Wynne Baxter lounge at the Amex.

The evening was hosted by Johnny Cantor from BBC Radio Sussex. On the podium taking fans' questions from the 300-odd supporters present were chief executive officer and deputy chairman Mr Paul Barber and head coach Mr Graham Potter.

It was a very informative event. We were given straight answers to everything asked, especially about the man with the black curly hair whose future seemed likely to dominate the evening.

In the end, only one question was put forward about Marc Cucurella and that came from host Johnny right at the start. Cucurella went on to be sold the following morning, making football history as the most expensive full back ever at a fee in excess of £54 million.

He was only with us a year and is now following his personal goals — to play Champions League football and hopefully make the Spanish World Cup Squad in November of this year.

You may remember that I was the one who raised the question of the failing lady's toilet in the East Upper on behalf of my wife during the January Fans' Forum. Thankfully, it was addressed ahead of the Amex hosting three games of the Women's Euros.

I did submit a question. There was no time for it to be covered, however, during the hour-long radio broadcast. It related to the big pitchside screens in the ground and whether, when budgets allow, additional ones could be hung on the West Stand and East Stand.

Along with new screens, I wanted to know if a timer clock could cover the minutes played in injury time. This might even assist the players on the pitch if they can see exactly how long is left. I stand to be corrected, of course!

So, to Sunday at Old Trafford. The sun shone and Johnny and Warren Aspinall treated us to a great photo on Twitter of them enjoying the Manchester weather before they began their commentary duties.

Sky decided that they would show us Manchester United winning 3-2 against Liverpool from 2010 before starting their live broadcast.

Of course, they were not going to show the last time United played Brighton, where we beat them 4-0 at the Amex in May.

United came out to warm up wearing training tops which made them look like Jokers from a set of playing cards. That was made to seem quite apt by the full-time whistle, at the same time as making the new Albion home shirt appear positively brilliant in comparison.

The headline news was that Cristiano Ronaldo was on the bench under new manager Erik ten Hag. Ronaldo eventually appeared at the start of the second half, but the Albion dealt with him very well and he made no difference to United's performance.

Don't get me wrong, he has been the best player in the world in the past. He does not look very happy with his current situation at Old Trafford and that seems to be impacting his performances. I am off to Madeira in September, so I will see if I can have a word about a fresh start for him at the Amex.

Ronaldo had barely taken his seat on the United bench when Brighton had the first chance of the game. Just 15 seconds in and Leandro Trossard hit David De Gea's side netting.

United settled after that and Albion did not have the possession they would normally like for the first eight to 10 minutes.

Bruno Fernandes should have scored when he sent a shot miles over the goal from a very good position. It was a terrible miss for a player of his quality and experience.

Danny Welbeck, Adam Lallana, Moises Caicedo, and Leandro Trossard helped to get Brighton on top after that. The positive, flowing football we had seen at the end of 2021-22 was back as if the Albion had not been on a summer break.

Erik ten Hag was realising what a big job he had on his hands. Looking even glummer were the Glazer family, sitting in the crowd and watching Pascal Gross take his record to six goals against United with a quick double.

Welbeck arrived on the left side after some superb football, working a cross in front of the United goal. Gross came in at the far post, making no mistake to put the Albion 1-0 up with 30 minutes played.

Next came the move of the match. Brighton appeared to be getting closed into their left back position until Trossard backheeled the ball out of there.

Caicedo had earlier survived a disgraceful stud-up challenge from Scott McTominay to carry the ball forward and find Gross.

Gross moved it to Lallana, Lallana found Solly March, and his low hard cross was pushed away by the hand of David De Gea. The ball ended up right at the feet of Gross who slotted home his second goal in nine minutes.

Old Trafford has seen some fantastic football in its time. Not many away teams will have scored a goal that good though. Brighton were making one of the most famous clubs in the world look positively poor.

We all know from many past experiences that no lead is safe against Manchester United. If they cannot find a way to comeback, then the officials will do it for them — even if the final whistle has already blown.

United also had Ronaldo to throw on. I was surprised that he was not introduced right away at the start of the second half.

Ronaldo's one contribution once he did enter came shortly after his introduction.

A low cross from the right reached Marcus Rashford, who nobody realised had been playing up to this point. Rashford connected with the ball well, but Robert Sanchez pulled off a world-class save to keep it out.

United were starting to come at Brighton now. They scored when Alexis Mac Allister was unlucky to put into his own net attempting to clear in a scramble from a corner. That set up a nervy last 20 minutes.

Christian Eriksen had a low shot which needed another great stop from Sanchez. Joel Veltman cleared when Sanchez spilled a ball in the danger zone. Lewis Dunk made a great sliding block as injury time beckoned.

The additional five minutes seemed to go on for an eternity. The Seagulls all kept their beaks up and ploughed on until the final whistle, securing a famous first-ever win at Old Trafford.

BBC Radio Sussex was full of fans praising Graham Potter and his squad afterwards and rightly so. The Albion continued where they had left off nine weeks ago when they ended 2021-22 with only one defeat from eight games.

If that form holds in 2022-23, we can look forward to an exciting season. Brighton showed United that a group working together in harmony is more effective than a set of talented, highly-paid individuals not willing to perform as a team.

There will be less successful days than this on the road ahead. When these come, just remember the feeling of winning 2-1 away at Man United.

Games like this are worth their weight in gold. And they make you proud to be an Albion supporter.

The Tony Bloom Documentary on Sky is a reminder of how lucky we are.

What a week it has been in the world of the Albion. The squad were quite rightly praised to the moon and back for their victory at Old Trafford last Sunday.

This turned out to be the start of a bad seven days for Manchester United. They bowed to the superior football of

Brentford on Saturday, despite putting better stats on the board than they had managed against Brighton.

Our own GP — not the doctor of course, but Graham Potter — was awarded the LMA Performance of the Week Award for overseeing Man United 1-2 Brighton performance.

Potter was voted the winner by a prestigious set of judges. Included on the panel were the likes of, Sir Alex Ferguson, Howard Wilkson, Les Ferdinand, and a certain Chris Hughton.

When accepting the award, Potter dedicated it to the entire squad and backroom staff who worked so hard to keep the show on the road. So, well done, Gaffer. Excellent work.

A few days after that historic first win away at Old Trafford, a 30-minute documentary landed on Sky Sports about the Albion.

When I watched, it made me realise just how much the club owes Mr Tony Bloom. It is quite clear that without his foresight and his financial input, Brighton would have been in an extremely awkward position when planning permission for the building of the Amex Stadium was received to go ahead.

The documentary about our chairman Mr Tony Bloom was broadcast twice in the week and I am sure it will run again soon. For anyone wanting to search for it, the Sky series is called Premier League Stories and the Brighton edition is simply titled *Tony Bloom*.

And one final announcement before we get to the opening home game of 2022-23 against Newcastle United. My book covering the 2021-22 season is now available on Amazon in both paperback and Kindle format. It is called, *Seagulls Best Ever Season Volume 1*.

I am also fortunate enough to be talking to Johnny Cantor on the Albion Unlimited Podcast this week about the book. The show went out on Tuesday evening, and you can listen on catch up through BBC Sounds.

Speaking of being fortunate, my wife and I felt lucky that we had booked onto the Seagull Travel Coach from Burgess Hill for the Newcastle fixture.

A fully air-conditioned mode of transport on such a scorching hot day was much needed. The only downside was that we arrived at the Amex as late as 2:15 p.m. There is not quite enough time to really take in the atmosphere and have a good mooch around. However, the comfort and service outweigh that.

Far from that famous old song "Walking in The Shade of The Old Apple Tree", we found ourselves "Walking in The Shade of The Old East Stand".

The sweeping structure of the Amex provided a respite from the beating sun. The players would have no such luck; they were in for a taxing afternoon.

Both teams emerged from the tunnel to the rapturous sounds of "Sussex by The Sea". A number of blue and white firework cannons went off from in front of the East Stand to get the season underway.

I found it quite strange seeing Dan Burn in his number 33 shirt playing for a different club. He seems happy with Newcastle, which is the main thing. I do hope though that when they inevitably splash more cash on players that Burn is not confined to the bench, however.

Brighton were straight into it, showing no signs of wilting in the heat. That is an indication of how fit Potter has his players, including the slightly older members of the squad.

Joel Veltman showed real grit and determination as he always does, navigating his way out of some really difficult situations to ensure Newcastle did not get the upper hand on his side of the pitch.

Leandro Trossard soon started to work his magic down the other flank to create a great chance for Danny Welbeck. His header was prevented from creeping into the net by Nick Pope, the England international goalkeeper that Newcastle have signed from Burnley.

That set the tone for Pope's afternoon. He made some excellent saves, which combined with good Newcastle defending was enough to see our visitors leave with a 0-0 draw.

Kieran Trippier just about managed to clear the ball off the line after Solly March got a shot away. From my seat in the East Upper, it looked to have gone in the net.

Goal line technology said otherwise, showing Trippier had kept it out by a quarter of the circumference of the football.

Newcastle did manage to get the ball into the back of the net at one point. The goal was ruled out though, as Callum Wilson had his boot over the head of Lewis Dunk, meaning the visiting striker was penalised for a high foot.

Next, it was the turn of Pascal Gross to create something. He fed into Adam Lallana who swivelled and hit a shot straight at Nick Pope.

As the half progressed and Pope kept saving from various Albion players, I began to think he was cramping our style. By all means, play like that for England at the World Cup if you are selected, but not when you are up against us at Brighton.

Just before half time and something unusual happened to Adam Webster; he lost a tackle. Miguel Almiron took advantage, racing away and feeding the ball to Wilson for a shot wonderfully kept out by Robert Sanchez before the offside flag went up.

0-0 at half time and Brighton had been the better side. Newcastle had managed some opportunities, but the stats showed the Albion to be playing well. A quick drink to refresh the players and then they could set about getting that breakthrough goal, right?

The second half started with a great passage of play by Brighton, working the ball up through the Newcastle half.

A beautifully floated cross was met by the head of Adam Lallana, who was again denied by Pope. Lallana is going to score again at some point in a Brighton shirt, I can feel it.

Pope next touched a Solly March shot over the crossbar and Dan Burn blocked a Welbeck shot. Burn came close to scoring at the other end with a header just over the bar and Veltman had to do more great defensive work to prevent Newcastle scoring.

The Albion kept battling on, continuing to give 120% despite the heat and Nick Pope. The time soon came for Potter to bring on Kaoru Mitoma for a Premier League debut and he entered with all guns blazing.

In the short time he was on the pitch, Mitoma showed real ball control and some great skill. He made some great runs down the left, cut inside really well, and was unlucky not to make contact with a pass into the six-yard box when more solid Newcastle defending intervened.

One Mitoma moment forced another Newcastle defender into clearing the ball off the goal line. By this point, I seemed to be up and down in my seat every couple of minutes whenever Mitoma was involved.

His next move down the left saw him drop a shoulder, drift inside and play a great pass to Pascal Gross who put the ball an arm's length wide, the exact sort of opportunity where he scored (twice) last week at Old Trafford. Such a shame that one did not go in.

Still, what a fantastic performance even if the result did not match it. Play like that against West Ham at the London Stadium and the Albion will have a chance of inflicting more misery on the Hammers, to go with the 3-1 Brighton win on the final day of last season.

We always seem to have luck on our side away at West Ham. There was little against Newcastle, so maybe it has all been saved for Sunday in the East End?

A decorating disaster made up for by two Brighton wins in a week.

Here is a quick tip for you. If you cannot get to an away game and find yourself with a few spare hours on your hands before Brighton kick off, do not start decorating.

On Sunday afternoon, I disconnected all the leads which keep the Noble household connected with the outside world and gambled that I could get a second coat of paint on the walls and wire everything back up in time for the game at West Ham.

It turned out to be an impossible task. In a rush to complete it, guess what happened? Yes, a tray of paint dropped everywhere.

The week did get better from there though. Brighton beat the Hammers and followed that up with a League Cup victory at Forest Green Rovers on Wednesday night. Two wins to make up for the decorating disaster. Can't be bad!

Whilst washing the paint off my hands before settling down to listen to the West Ham game on BBC Radio Sussex, I was hit by a longing to be at the London Stadium.

Not just because it would have meant no paint spillage, but because there is a little bit of history between West Ham United and Tony Noble.

I know what you are thinking — is he related to Mark Noble? Not as far as I know. However, my dad was born in East London a few streets away from Upton Park and as a boy of course he was a West Ham supporter.

He took me up there one day and we bought a West Ham

pendant from Bobby Moore's sports shop. It was signed by Moore, Geoff Hurst, and Martin Peters and would be worth a small fortune these days.

I placed it for safekeeping inside a book and there it stayed. Which book I could never remember, and as my dad was not a hoarder like myself, it must have been thrown away at some point.

That still bugs me as I remember so well the World Cup of 1966 having been a 10-year-old boy when Moore, Hurst, and Peters helped England win the cup.

Maybe we will see a Brighton player help England to their second World Cup this November? Former Brighton coach Paul Nevin is now at West Ham and helps out with England.

He can surely report back to Gareth Southgate the great form Lewis Dunk is in having witnessed it firsthand on Sunday. Just maybe we see Dunk in Harry Maguire's spot come November in Qatar?

The big news when the teams were announced was that Neal Maupay was on the Albion bench. There was no further hint over whether he will be moving or not, although the fact he did not feature at Forest Green in midweek suggests he will.

Warren Aspinall reported that the grass at the London Stadium looked long and unwatered. I know we have a major water shortage, but the lack of watering must have been down to West Ham trying to make it more difficult for the Albion to carry out their slick passing than wanting to help Thames Water save supplies.

Lukasz Fabianski was wearing a bright yellow goalkeeper's top and bright orange loves, which the commentator likened to a Solero ice cream.

I was hoping that he would melt like one in the sun, to give our strikers a chance. Rather it was Thilo Kehrer who melted, as the German defender gave away a penalty and Brighton the chance to take the lead.

A 20th-minute break allowed Leandro Trossard to race up the pitch. He had Danny Welbeck ahead of him and slipped a slide rule pass through, causing Kehrer to make a challenge right on the edge of the box.

Referee Anthony Taylor was there and had no doubt as to whether it was a penalty. He awarded it straight away. There was a short wait as Warren told us they had to wake up the officials at Stockley Park from their afternoon nap to review the action.

They eventually concurred with Mr Taylor. That two-minute wait must have seemed like an age for Alexis Mac Allister, who we were told hugged the ball in anticipation of taking the penalty.

It was a cracker. He played it to the right-hand corner. Fabianski went the wrong way and Brighton had the lead against West Ham in yet another game.

As a listener, it did not sound as if the Hammers were giving the Albion much of a problem in the run-up to half time. I returned to the decorating when the whistle went for the 15-minute break, quickly checking the Leeds v Chelsea score.

The paint nearly went flying again in surprise that Leeds were 2-0 up at half time. It ended 3-0 and I wondered how poor Marc Cucurella found his first experience of the short end of Thomas Tuchel's short fuse.

Apparently, part of the problem was that Chelsea had no airplane to get to Leeds on Saturday, so they had to get the bus. Well, if that's how it works, we have real hope.

No real decorating got done before it was back to the game. I felt sure the Irons would come out all guns blazing. They had a couple of opportunities, but the Albion seemed to have them covered.

The 63rd minute saw Adam Lallana substituted to allow the Brighton debut of new signing Pervis Estupinan. He helped get the Albion back on the front foot and within three minutes of coming on, Brighton scored again.

A delightful flick on by Pascal Gross put Trossard on course with Fabianski, who he beat with ease. The assist from Gross was something else.

Then came the push from West Ham. David Moyes made his five changes but not even that could help the Irons find a way through the Albion.

The final whistle saw the players celebrate in front of the away fans with Graham Potter punching the air. I was more subdued in my celebrations at home, having spilt more paint than I had actually painted on the walls.

By Wednesday night, the decorating was done. There were no dramas and I sat down to listen to the Forest Green game, coming live from the greenest football club in the land.

Everything is recycled, even the seats you sit on to watch a game. A tweeted photo of our commentators Johnny Cantor and Warren showed them squashed in like sardines into this small League One ground.

Then guess what? The connection was lost for just a few minutes at the start of the game. Johnny told listeners it may happen again as there was not enough room for all their radio kit. I think he and Warren Aspinall wanted to eat another vegan pie, that are so popular at this football club apparently.

Potter made 11 changes, giving us the chance to get a good look at new signings and young players. Jason Steele captained the Albion in goal.

In front of him came Levi Colwill, Jan Paul van Hecke, and Ed Turns. Midfield was Tariq Lamptey, Jack Spong, Steve Alzate, and Kaoru Mitoma. Then the front three of Julio Enciso, Deniz Undav, and Evan Ferguson.

Johnny and Warren described Brighton as sloppy in the final third during the opening 30 minutes. The commentary team wanted the Albion to move the ball a lot quicker.

Maybe that was part of the problem? The balls being used in this competition are Football League balls rather than Premier League balls. The players do train with them to get used to the difference, but it could have had an impact and explain the slow start to the game.

Any questions about the balls were extinguished on 38 minutes. Undav slotted home his first goal of hopefully many in a Brighton shirt to put the Albion 1-0 ahead.

The young Brighton team were starting to settle now. A second was scored in the first of two minutes of injury time. Alzate used his weaker left foot to let rip a shot that went straight into the back of the net from distance.

Steele made a great save to prevent Forest Green Rovers from getting a goal back shortly after the restart. That served as a reminder of the threat they could offer and encouraged Brighton to get back on top.

A great run from Evan Ferguson down the right saw him deliver a cross which Denis Undav headed wide of the far post. Undav seemed to know that was a real chance for him.

Then to finish the evening off nicely, a perfect long ball was hit down the left side for substitute James Furlong to latch onto. He did well to cross to Ferguson who slotted home right on the final whistle.

The third-round draw has paired Brighton with Arsenal. That will be interesting. I have just been watching the Arsenal documentary on Amazon Prime and Mikel Arteta seems desperate to win a trophy. Will Arteta play his first team against us at the Emirates? Well, we will find out in November.

Those Leeds fans who put one finger up to our coach got the score right

It is all go for football fans at the moment. The games are coming thick and fast, with Leeds the latest visitors to the Amex on another sunny Saturday afternoon.

We all knew this would be a keenly contested match as games against Leeds always are. The visitors were coming off the back of a 3-0 win over Chelsea and a midweek cup success.

Jesse Marsch the Leeds manager has them playing well and confidence in the Leeds camp would have been high. It was great to see Brighton playing their hearts out, edging it 1-0. With a bit more luck, it would have been a more convincing victory.

Our journey this week involved the Seagull Travel Coach from Lindfield. We use Seagull Travel on occasion and the decision was another good one as we enjoyed an air-conditioned coach rather than a crushed train.

There was a bit of confusion beforehand as not many Albion supporters seemed to know where the coach was stopping.

It turns out that Seagull Travel have changed the route to the stadium. Rumour has it that next week for the Leicester City game, the normal way via Lewes will be reinstated. Still a cushty ride into the Amex, however.

Here is hoping. Had our driver not displayed some quick thinking on the way, then we would not have arrived at the Amex until after 2.30 p.m.

It was a little bumpy driving over that central reservation, but worth it in the end. (That is a joke by the way, just in case anyone at Seagull Travel is reading and thinking our driver went off-piste!)

We got chatting on the coach to a fellow Brighton fan who sits with his wife in the East Lower. He said that during the 0-0 draw with Newcastle, he put his programme over his arm to try and prevent getting burnt as the suncream he had on was not strong enough.

What he did not expect when he removed the programme sometime later was that the heat combined with the pre-match fireworks display would have transferred the ink onto his arm.

He found himself with the front cover of the programme tattooed onto his skin. It washed off when he got home, which was unfortunate as it looked like one of those designer tattoos people pay good money for. And he had it for free.

It will not be long until we are arriving at the Amex in pouring rain and heavy wind. The idea of a programme melting onto a man's arm will seem a million miles away then.

Interrupting our conversation on the way down the A23 was a bus full of Leeds fans, who our coach became involved in with a lot of overtaking.

Every time we passed each other, the Leeds fans would show us one finger. How clever of them to predict that Brighton would win the game 1-0. That is what it meant, right?

The only downside of going to games via a coach is you very occasionally arrive a little late due to heavy traffic which cannot be helped. On this occasion I barely had enough time to buy my Albion Wine Gums. However, it was straight down to business.

Perhaps that is something the club and Seagull Travel can look at. I daresay the Albion would want people arriving earlier to get a drink and a sausage.

I like to get there in plenty of time to soak up a matchday atmosphere. The feel of the crowd. The smell of burgers and fish & chips. The feel of a freshly printed programme (before it gets tattooed onto your arm). The sound of the visiting fans chanting in the South Stand.

Then into our East Upper seats to the music of Elton John & Dua Lipa whilst Robert Sanchez, Jason Steele and goalkeeper coach Ben Roberts warm up in front of the North Stand.

Then along skip both Gully & Sally. The two giant seagulls that always make me laugh. It is, in fact, my dream job. One day, just maybe they will let me dress up as Gully. OMG, I would be over the moon!

There was another large pyrotechnic display before kick-off. Hopefully, nobody had their programmes touching their skin. I did wonder what my new friend from the East Lower was doing.

Leeds supporters were in great voice, as were our own North

Stand. Even the East Stand was singing along, which was great to hear. The flying start the Albion have made to the season has clearly got everyone really excited.

Straight from the kick-off, it appeared that Leeds's tactics were to make silly fouls to stop Brighton playing. One of these fouls was on Solly March, who was grabbed around the throat by Diego Llorente and pulled down on the right side of the pitch.

Another foul led to Pascal Gross floating over a beautiful free kick for Adam Webster. Webster took it well, however, the header passed Illan Meslier's right-hand post.

Pervis Estupinan was enjoying an encouraging Amex debut. He looks like a promising talent who can help fill the void left by Marc Cucurella departing for Chelsea.

March on the other side of the pitch to Estupinan was having a great game. Some fine midfield control from Alexis MacAllister saw the ball played out to the right to March whose shot was saved by Meslier.

Leandro Trossard had a good chance from the resulting corner, but he could not keep the volley down as it went over the bar.

Most of the attacking football seemed to be coming from the Albion. March was again denied by Meslier, and the rebound cleared away from the Leeds goal.

Then March was fouled again down that right side, this time by Marc Roca. Another free kick was beautifully placed by Gross to Webster who headed it wide. Never mind Adam, it will come — give it time, I say!

Leeds had offered only very little on the break and I felt a Brighton goal was coming. The second half began with Gross just a second too late to convert an Estupinan cross. The build-up to that chance was great, involving Danny Welbeck and Pervis Estupinan.

Pascal Gross played a real peach of a through ball into the path of Solly March. He accelerated away, going one-on-one against Meslier once again.

Unfortunately for March, Meslier saved the ball to deny him a goal. Like Webster, March is another player who just needs to keep trying for it to come good.

Webster did some attacking next, crossing the ball to the left where Trossard was. Trossard passed to Estupinan and his great cross fell to Solly March. Sadly, it was not to be March's day as the ball flew right over the bar.

An error from Pervis Estupinan at the other end gave Leeds a golden opportunity to score. Somehow, they put the ball wide of an open goal from yards away. Can anything beat that when it comes to the miss of the season? We will have to wait and see.

Brighton became a little nervous after that, as Leeds had several attempts. It needed our Doc GP to settle the players, which he did to help the Albion take the lead.

The move started with a series of passes out from the back. Lewis Dunk to Estupinan, through to Welbeck laying off to Caicedo who feeds Trossard to square to Gross.

Gross does not pass up the chance, striking low and hard to Meslier's left to make it Brighton 1-0 Leeds United. There was a wait whilst VAR at Stockley Park checked for an offside. Once it was confirmed as being a legal goal, we were able to celebrate a second time around.

Marsch felt this was all unfair and soon his remonstrations with the referee earned him a yellow card. That caused things to get a little heated with Webster drawing a yellow card. Leeds put the free kick that Adam Webster had conceded narrowly wide of the far post.

Brighton were hanging on a bit, to the point that I felt a little sorry for those in the North Stand. Apart from the goal, all the action in both halves had taken place at the opposite end of the ground with the Albion dominating the first half and then Leeds better in the second.

The Seagulls were the ones who got the result they wanted when the full-time whistle blew. Brighton finished the weekend in fourth spot with 10 points from 12 so far.

We even enjoyed a brief few minutes at the top of the Premier League after that Gross goal. I wonder if that might also be what the Leeds fans meant when giving us all the finger, that Brighton would be number one? They are a visionary bunch.

Not even Glenn Murray doing punditry could bring Brighton luck

The games keep coming thick and fast. Tuesday evening saw Brighton play for the fourth time in ten days, this time away at Fulham on the banks of the River Thames.

Not being able to make the trip to Craven Cottage, I took a two-prong approach to keeping up. This involved tuning in to watch pictures from the Cottage on an app whilst listening to the BBC Radio Sussex commentary of Johnny Cantor and Warren Aspinall.

We all knew that victory would make Brighton overnight Premier League leaders for the first time ever. Standing in our way was a certain Aleksandar Mitrovic.

How our defenders dealt with him was always going to decide the outcome. Unfortunately, it was Mitrovic who came out on top. There was no shame in that, he is a fantastic player.

Speaking of fantastic players, Glenn Murray was doing punditry on BT Sport. How great to hear him refer to Brighton as "we" when talking about the Albion.

If not even having the Seagulls record scorer cheering on from the touchline could provide Brighton with good luck, then maybe it was never meant to be our night.

An ominous sign was the storm clouds gathering before kick-off. They created a beautiful scene above Craven Cottage.

There was no rain from those clouds, but that did not prevent a couple of Albion players losing their footing and slipping on the turf.

Fulham had the first chance when Bobby Decordova-Reid put in an early cross which Mitrovic could not quite get onto to slot home.

Joel Veltman needed thanking once again for putting the ball behind for a corner. Robert Sanchez had to make a great stop from the corner with Brighton eventually getting a free kick.

When Pascal Gross slipped, he managed to turn it into a pass. Leandro Trossard was the recipient, and his cross from the left was headed wide at full pace and power by Solly March.

The halfway stage was reached with the score still at 0-0 and not many clearcut chances. It had been a real battle in the first half.

I thought Fulham were perhaps the better side. They chased everything, looked fast, and moved the ball around quickly. The Albion had not clicked as they have done this season.

Early in the second half and Moises Caicedo fouled Kenny Tete. It was one of those aerial duels where both players were watching the ball and neither intended to impede the other.

Fulham though got a free kick, cleared behind by Adam Webster. I felt nervous whenever the hosts had a set piece, knowing what Mitrovic can do in the air.

However, Fulham took the corner short to Andreas Pereira. His cross was poor, but Fulham remained in possession and Neeskens Kebano played in another cross.

This one went right across the goal and guess what? Mitrovic slid it home at the far post to put the Cottagers 1-0 up.

Never mind, I thought. There were still 42 minutes left for Brighton to fight back. The Albion set about doing that by winning a corner.

Of all the things that could have happened from that play, Fulham breaking to score again was the last thing Brighton would have wanted.

Lewis Dunk looked like he was trying to break the land speed record to get back and break up the Cottagers' counter.

When Pereira crossed, Dunk was going too fast to stop and he ended up catching the ball with his right foot. Sanchez was wrong-footed and the ball sped into the back of the net.

I felt really sorry for both Lewis Dunk and Robert Sanchez. It was one of those things neither could do much about. And Brighton trailed 2-0 because of it with 55 minutes played on the clock.

You know as well as I do that the Albion never give up. They continued to play their hearts out. Nice play down the left and into the 18-yard box saw Pervis Estupinan and Gross go down.

Referee Thomas Bramall — on his Premier League debut — allowed play to continue. Webster picked the ball up on the right and put it out of play, alerting Mr Bramall that Estupinan was still on the ground and in a lot of pain.

That seemed to wake the team up at Stockley Park and they told Mr Bramall to have a look at the incident again. Estupinan had been kicked on the calf by Decordova-Reid and Brighton had a penalty.

Alexis Mac Allister seemed to know the outcome before anyone else. He stood there with the ball in his arms waiting to take the penalty.

The wait must have felt like an eternity. When Mac Allister did get the chance, he concentrated on the ball and rifled it to the left of Bernd Leno.

An hour had been played and Brighton were back in the game. We were nearly out of it again when Sanchez had a moment, spilling the ball over the top of his head.

Kebano was right there but somehow missed the open goal by firing over the crossbar. *Phew, what a let off,* I thought — along with urging Sanchez to switch on.

Kaoru Mitoma, Danny Welbeck, and Tariq Lamptey soon came on. Mitoma did some great work to create a chance for Trossard but his good low shot was saved by Leno.

Another series of moves gave Deniz Undav a chance. Welbeck chipped into Undav and he hit Leno's post with Welbeck just unable to slot it home on the rebound and level the scoreline.

There were six minutes of injury time, but Brighton did not have another chance. The final whistle brought with it the first defeat of the season for the Albion.

Our position in the table did not change though. The Albion remain fourth with 10 points. The longer we can stay in that top group, the better, as it means we are heading towards our first target of 40 points.

Thankfully, we will face Mitrovic only once more this season. This Sunday it is Leicester City, who are yet to win a game. Let us hope we can keep it that way!

CHAPTER 2
SEPTEMBER 2022

Brighton 5-2 Leicester was a day that will live in infamy.

AS FRANKLIN D ROOSEVELT said back in 1941, "A day that will live in infamy." To see the Albion, play to such a level and score five goals in a topflight game for the first time ever was a real privilege, not an infamous act!

The day started with another smooth ride from Seagull Travel on the Lindfield coach. We arrived at the Amex with 50 minutes to spare before kick-off, thanks to some great driving by the coach driver.

There was just one holdup in the depths of mid Sussex — caused by somebody riding a rickshaw of all things. A rickshaw cycling around the back roads of Sussex is not particularly safe, especially with no overtaking opportunities and a lack of Highway Code rules for bicycles in general, let alone rickshaws.

We eventually made it past the rickety rickshaw. Our only other unusual encounter following that was some parrots. I had never seen parrots on this route before in Mid Sussex, just like how I had never seen Brighton score five times in a Premier League game. Quite an eye-opener, really on the way to the game.

Leicester arrived at the Amex having had a troubled start to the 2022-23 season. They sat bottom of the table, with one draw and four defeats from five matches.

The Leicester owners wrote to fans via their matchday programme earlier in the week, saying funds were not available to spend on improving their squad.

This situation was commented on by Brendan Rodgers following the Foxes' midweek defeat to Manchester United.

Rodgers is a well-respected coach who has taken Leicester to great things, similar to the job our own Graham Potter is doing.

Leicester made the perfect start to what ended up being 100 minutes of entertaining play. If you were still in the loo, buying Albion sweets or finishing a pint and not in your seat for kick-off, then you would have missed the Foxes take the lead after 53 seconds.

Even those who were in position would have missed it if they blinked. *Oh my God*, I thought. This afternoon might be tougher than the league table suggested.

Had all the photo shoots involving the players right before kick-off distracted them too much from the task ahead?

Both Leicester goals came from uncharacteristic mistakes from the Albion. For the lads to battle back and find a way to win in convincing fashion even after the errors was a result of them playing their hearts out, running for every ball, and not letting anything beat them.

Youri Tielemans crowded out Solly March, winning the ball to feed Harvey Barnes. He passed to Patson Daka who squared across goal from the west side of the pitch to the east where Kelechi Iheanacho was lurking to make it 1-0.

Brighton were not deterred. A few minutes later and a Pascal Gross cross from the right was returned into the box by Leandro Trossard on the left.

It found March, who headed into the Leicester goal. Or did he? It turned out that the ball had caught Luke Thomas on its way in, and so it was credited as an own goal. The stadium erupted and suddenly things felt right in the world again with Brighton on level terms.

March ended up winning the sponsor's man-of-the-match award. I felt it could have gone to anyone. A team award would have been more fitting by full-time; as March said in his post-match interview, this is the best squad he has ever played with in his 10 years now at the Albion.

It did not take long after Solly March (or Thomas for Leicester) equalised until Brighton took the lead again. Enock Mwepu swept through the middle of the park, heading straight for the Leicester goal.

He was flanked on either side by Danny Welbeck on the left

and Moises Caicedo on the right. Mwepu opted to go right to Caicedo, who hit a right-footed shot across Danny Ward and inside the far post.

The clock was showing just 15 minutes played and already we had seen three goals. In the 33rd minute, we had a fourth as Leicester made it 2-2.

Tielemans played a lobbed ball over the top to find Daka in the middle. Lewis Dunk and Joel Veltman were caught on either side of Daka with neither able to prevent him from controlling the ball and beating Sanchez right-footed.

However, disappointing it was to concede again, we were at least treated to a display of gymnastics from Daka in the celebration which was of Olympic standard.

The Foxes clearly had a lot of fight to go with the backflips and cartwheels of Daka. It was obvious that Brighton would need to dig deep in the second half to take all three points.

Dig deep and produce some quality they certainly did. Alexis Mac Allister duly provided the latter by scoring one of the goals of the season.

A Pascal Gross free kick was cleared back to the edge of the penalty area. Mac Allister hit a powerful volley from 30 yards that flew into the back of the net.

Wild celebrations took place all around the Amex at this fantastic piece of skill and wonderful finish. That was until somebody at Stockley Park woke up and decided to take a look at a replay.

Four minutes later and VAR told referee Tony Harrington to go and look at the pitch side monitor. Mwepu had been a millimetre offside when Gross took the original free kick and so the goal was ruled out.

Brighton kept going and they soon had a legal third. Mac Allister started the move, getting the ball to Gross on a right angle to the box.

Gross carved a pass through the Leicester defence to Trossard, who turned inside and hit a left-footed shot that slid in at the far post. The Albion led 3-2.

The Amex crowd suddenly became greedy. We wanted more goals. We felt like Brighton could score more, at the same time as wondering whether Leicester would launch another comeback.

Trossard felt the mood and soon earned the Albion a penalty.

He ran along the goal line, keeping the ball in play and drawing a foul from Wilfred Ndidi.

Once again, we had a lengthy wait for VAR to check out what had happened. Eventually, Mac Allister was allowed to take the penalty and he hammered it down the middle with Ward diving right.

Mac Allister normally goes for the right-hand corner, so Ward had clearly done his homework. Mac Allister was clever enough to change things up and Brighton were 4-2 ahead as a result.

All those VAR delays meant we had seven minutes of stoppage time. Tariq Lamptey, Pervis Estupinan, Deniz Undav, and new signing from Chelsea Billy Gilmour were all on hoping to help the Albion find a fifth.

Brighton eventually secured that history-making goal in the final seconds with a world-class free-kick into the top corner by, yes, Alexis Mac Allister. He was not to be denied something spectacular.

Potter and the players deserve our thanks. They are providing incredible memories and fantastic days out for us supporters. I hope that they are enjoying it all as much as we are.

The players play the game — and these Brighton players are great.

I am sure many fans feel a little lost right now, as I do. It has been a whirlwind two weeks, and nobody seems entirely sure where we are at the present time.

However, with the dust settled now on Graham Potter's departure to Chelsea, there are 'Reasons to be Cheerful' as Ian Dury and The Blockheads sang a while back.

A fresh chapter may be about to begin for Brighton in a new era under new manager Roberto De Zerbi. Thankfully though, we still have the two constants in our midst — Mr Tony Bloom and Mr Paul Barber. They will guide the Albion onwards and upwards.

Like many of you, I was really disappointed in Potter leaving his job, it was not yet finished. It just goes to show that no matter what people say about long-term projects and ambitions, you can never believe what you hear.

Money talks folks, but we all know that. Take away the disappointment and you can never blame an ambitious person for wanting to better themselves or wanting to secure a financial future for their family.

Think about it who in their right mind would turn down any job with the financial package of £12 million a year which was offered to Graham Potter?

Even if he cannot work his magic at Stamford Bridge and ends up being sacked long before his five-year contract ends, he will get a very nice payoff to spend shopping in Waitrose whilst on gardening leave.

I personally wish Potter well, knowing that the foundations he laid at Brighton and with the Albion squad will remain with the players even after his departure.

Throughout my career spanning many years, I have been fortunate to have worked under many good managers. . . and a few not-so-good ones.

Under the not-so-good-ones, we all tend to coast along not doing our best. Under the good ones, people learn and improve, and it benefits their abilities and careers.

Graham Potter has had a positive impact on all the players he has worked with. He has taught them to believe in themselves and helped them to levels good enough to be flying high in the Premier League table.

It is those players who play the game, not the manager. And this Brighton squad is full of great players. There is no reason whatsoever why they will not continue to do this under Signor De Zerbi the same way they did at the back end of 2021-22 and in the first six games of the new season.

Brighton do not play again until going to Anfield at the start of October. The short break due to the loss of our dear Queen, the Crystal Palace game being postponed due to a planned rail strike, and the international break came at an ideal time really for Albion.

It will allow the players and Roberto De Zerbi the chance to readjust and apply themselves for six more weeks of football leading up to the World Cup in November.

Another sign of how good these Brighton players are is that a number of them will be in Qatar, doing us proud. We wish them every success, of course.

It does not seem like Lewis Dunk will be going with England. I was disappointed not to see Gareth Southgate bring our captain into the squad in place of Harry Maguire, who has spent more time on the bench this season than I have on my office chair.

Talking of England, one former international has really stepped up to the mark for Brighton since Potter's departure. Adam Lallana has put his experience and leadership skills to good use, coming in for praise from Mr Barber.

With individuals like Adam Lallana still on board, there are people to continue to install into the players what Potter taught them. Along with the ideas of Roberto De Zerbi, of course.

We know that the Albion never give up. They fight until the last whistle is blown. Now is the time to start getting excited about how this new chapter pans out when our beloved Brighton restart the season with enthused ambition and effort.

Good luck to the players, De Zerbi, and one final message for Potter — hands off cherry picking our team in the January transfer window.

CHAPTER 3
October 2022

New beginning for Brighton provides reasons for excitement.

SITTING DOWN TO write about Liverpool 3-3 Brighton and it feels like an absolute age since we last saw the Albion in Premier League action.

Enough drama has happened to fill a year, as we have read about on the news. And yet it is only just four weeks ago that we were basking in a record-breaking 5-2 win over Leicester City in the sunshine at the Amex Stadium.

Winston Churchill was always good for an amazing quote. One of his most famous I think sums up how many of us feel about the Albion as Graham Potter gives way to Robert De Zerbi.

"Now, this is not the end. It is not even the beginning of the end. But it is perhaps the end of the beginning."

Potter has started the Albion on their journey. His part is done. Now we watch the Seagulls fly to new heights with the confidence installed by Graham Potter and the further guidance of Roberto De Zerbi.

Before the teams walked out into the Anfield sunshine, there was a sense this would be a special afternoon. I could feel it over the airwaves, listening to BBC Radio Sussex.

"You'll Never Walk Alone" was drowned out on the radio by chants of "Albion, Albion". Everyone was fully behind De Zerbi and the players, who we must remember are the same ones who have carried Brighton into fourth spot. It was not all about Potter.

Roberto De Zerbi stuck with almost the same team as had played in the Leicester game. The only change was Pervis

Estupinan coming in for Enock Mwepu, who has spent time in hospital with sickness after the international break.

Straight from kick-off and the Albion were determined to impress their new head coach. That led to a goal with only four minutes played, what a start for Roberto De Zerbi.

It was a great little one-two and back flick from Danny Welbeck which gave Leandro Trossard the chance to place the ball into the right-hand side of Alisson's goal.

If my settee springs thought they would be in for a rest from celebrations in the lounge now Potter had left, they were sorely mistaken!

Liverpool tried to respond with some fast breaks led by Mo Salah. The Albion did well to keep them at bay, although Robert Sanchez had one lucky escape. He was a little too casual with the ball at his feet and lost out to Salah. Thankfully, the ball went out for a goal kick. *Steady Robert*, I thought!

Welbeck nearly put Brighton 2-0 up with a header from a Solly March cross. Alisson made the save, something which would become a theme of the game. Welbeck though showed he was on the prowl and looking for that first goal of the season.

Brighton continued to put a lot of pressure on Liverpool. Eventually, a second goal came. March produced a nice touch to Trossard, and he did the rest. The Albion led 2-0 with just 18 minutes played.

I always love listening to Warren Aspinall's analysis. He never misses a thing. Warren thought Brighton should have been 4-0 up rather than just two and that the movement of the forwards was causing real problems for Liverpool.

He also told us that De Zerbi was pushing the back three well up the field, sometimes into the opposition's half. Warren said he would not have liked to play in this team with how fit the players needed to be to get back in case of a speedy break.

It sounded as if Brighton were playing at a very fast pace, quicker to everything that a slow and sluggish Liverpool seemed to be displaying.

A yellow card for Pervis Estupinan timewasting could not derail the Albion, nor could Mo Salah when a combination of Sanchez and Lewis Dunk denied the Liverpool marksman a goal.

The hosts managed to strike back before half time. An offside flag went up against Salah as he slipped the ball back to Roberto Firmino, breaking to finish between Dunk and Adam Webster.

VAR looked and decided that Salah had not been offside. It was the correct decision but one Brighton would not have wanted. With their tails up, you felt Liverpool would now become the dangerous opponents we know they can be.

The Albion made it to the break without conceding again. Brighton were no longer defending the Kop after the interval, suggesting that Dunk won the toss.

Liverpool always like to attack their own fans in the second half, hoping that the noise from that end of the ground can suck the ball over the line.

Not that attacking the opposite end made much difference. Jurgen Klopp had clearly had words and the Reds equalised within nine minutes of the game restarting.

A swift, accurate ball from Jordan Henderson found substitute Luis Diaz. He made an instant impact, crossing to Firmino to slot home his second of the afternoon.

Gulp. Now Brighton were in trouble. Liverpool's momentum carried them into the lead on 63 minutes when an unfortunate incident occurred.

Sanchez committed himself to punching the ball away from a well-placed corner, only to completely miss it. Instead, the ball hit the back of Webster and went straight into the Albion net.

That left Brighton with 27 minutes plus injury time to try and find an equaliser. Not many would have been expecting the Seagulls to manage it, certainly not the Anfield crowd.

They were silenced on 83 minutes via a brilliant passing move. Webster started it, sliding the ball to Welbeck who worked it out wide to March and then to Kaoru Mitoma.

Substitute Mitoma got to the line and crossed to the back post where Trossard was waiting to slot it home. An amazing comeback and even more amazing, a hat-trick for Leandro Trossard!

De Zerbi danced a little jig on the sideline in celebration. It seems to have been shown in every highlights package of the game. You could see how excited he was for his players.

There were a few heart-in-mouth moments after that. The worst was right at the end when Welbeck gave away a free kick some 30 yards out.

Alexander-Arnold hit a cracker, but Sanchez got a slight touch on it to send the ball around the post and prevent Liverpool from making it 4-3.

If every game under Roberto De Zerbi is to be this exciting, I expect I will need to get used to my heart pounding on a much more regular basis.

Roll on Spurs at the Amex on Saturday to find out.

The Spurs dig in pays a compliment to Brighton.

We were blessed with a lovely sunny Saturday afternoon but no trains to the Amex for Brighton v Spurs. A huge number of Albion supporters overcame the travel problems but unfortunately, the team were not able to do likewise to a stubborn Spurs defence.

Look at the stats afterwards and you see just how much Tottenham dug in. Antonio Conte decided the best way to beat Brighton was by defending, even though Spurs have the scoring talents of Harry Kane and Son Heung-min. Playing that way is a big compliment to the Albion.

Trains and Tottenham defending were not the only problems. There were reportedly very few buses to get people to and from the Amex and local roads were understandably extremely busy.

The early bird catches the worm and so I set out at 2.50 p.m. from North Sussex to ensure an early arrival time at the Amex, a bowl of chips, and a look around the Seagulls Superstore.

This was a moment of great pride for me as my first book about last season was now being stocked in the club shop. A schoolboy dream had come true.

Any game against a Conte team is tough. Spurs had added motivation following a dreadful blow in the week, the death of their 61-year-old fitness coach Gian Piero Ventrone.

A one-minute applause was held before kick-off for Ventrone and the grief in the Spurs squad was evident on the faces of the players and Conte. Both sides wore black armbands out of respect.

It was also the Premier League's "No to Racism" weekend. All players took a knee before kick-off, one of the games this season when the gesture will be observed. It was greeted with the normal fantastic applause from fans.

From the kick-off, it was obvious that Spurs were going to

give a better performance than those seen against Arsenal and Eintracht Frankfurt. Brighton started slowly in contrast, with misplaced passes in midfield and giving the ball away too easily in other areas causing a few issues.

The Albion seemed to have less space than normal. Tottenham were always in the right place at the right time, closing our players down through relentless running. A fitting tribute to Ventrone's work as fitness coach.

There was an early error from the match officials when Matt Doherty claimed a corner and they went with his appeal. Eventually, the correct decision of goal kick was made.

Doherty then placed a good cross from Ryan Sessegnon over the bar. Brighton had their first chance next, Danny Welbeck hitting a low shot only about a foot wide of Hugo Lloris' post after the Albion sliced through the Tottenham midfield.

Kane was booked for a clear piece of cheating when he used his right hand to push the ball into his path as he rushed towards the Albion goal.

Robert Sanchez had to use his hands next — legally, of course, as the goalkeeper — to brilliantly keep out a rocket from Rodrigo Bentancur following a good Son run.

It was Son's cross that provided Spurs with their goal halfway through the first half. Kane lowered his body to the ground and helped it into the back of the net with a clever finish. VAR checked but there was nothing wrong and Tottenham led 1-0.

A certain Yves Bissouma joined Kane in the book with a really bad tackle on Alexis Mac Allister. It was totally unnecessary and quite rightly earned Bissouma a yellow card.

Brighton had some good chances to equalise before half time. Lewis Dunk nearly converted a corner but he was just unable to get over the top of the ball with his header.

A cracking shot from Solly March then flew just wide of the post. Roberto De Zerbi has said he wants to see March score more goals and I am sure it will happen for him soon.

Lloris made a good save from Welbeck as the Albion finished the half strongly. Now it was time to see if the new manager could install further enthusiasm in the players and find a way through the stubborn Spurs defence.

March was very active down the right early in the second

half, putting some great crosses into the box which Spurs had to deal with.

Brighton's momentum was broken a little when Joel Veltman was booked for a tackle on Son which he was in total control of and won the ball.

To make matters worse, Dunk picked up a yellow for the same incident as he pointed out to referee Tony Harrington what a terrible decision had just been made.

Some indecision in the Albion defence gave Kane a chance which he should have scored. De Zerbi decided that made it time for a change and on came Kaoru Mitoma.

He was quickly into the action with some of those left-wing charges which Brighton fans have already fallen in love with.

Mitoma is such an exciting player to watch; every time he gets the ball you expect something is going to happen.

Spurs fans probably feel similar about Son. He took a free kick which was headed just past the post, causing Sanchez to produce one of his cat-like dives just in case.

Son beat Sanchez with his next effort, a cracking shot that flew into the back of the net. It was very clearly offside however and so the goal was correctly ruled out.

Welbeck fizzed one past the post for another near miss as the game prepared to enter its final 10 minutes. Brighton have been so good at scoring late goals that I still believed an equaliser would be found before the full-time whistle.

There were a couple more valiant efforts from the Albion but none which ended with the ball slotted past Lloris.

A first home defeat of the season was no disaster and a quick chance to bounce back at Brentford on a Friday night, presuming we can keep Ivan Toney quiet.

Bees excellence at both ends should not leave Albion downhearted.

Things do not seem to be going Brighton's way at the moment. Last week started with the sad news that the Albion's number eight, Enock Mwepu had been forced into retirement with a hereditary heart condition.

The issue was discovered during the international break. We

were informed that when Mwepu returned home, he spent some more time in hospital in Sussex where the condition was diagnosed.

Enock Mwepu will be a huge loss for the Albion. How popular he is was shown by the way at Friday evening's game at the Gtech Stadium against Brentford became a tribute to Mwepu.

The Sky TV broadcast began with Brighton chief executive Mr Paul Barber on our screens, expressing his sincere good wishes for Enoch Mwepu.

Mr Barber reiterated that Mwepu would receive all the help and assistance needed from the club to help him start a new career.

We were later shown our chairman Mr Tony Bloom watching the action from the away end. He appeared to be enjoying himself, despite the result.

You do not see many owners of Premier League football clubs mixing with fans in this way. What a great honour for those at Brentford to get to watch the match alongside the chairman — who presumably did not have the sort of access issues at the turnstiles that other prominent Albion supporters experienced!

Brentford have not lost a Friday night game at the Gtech Stadium for quite a while. The Bees seem to love playing at home under the lights and this was no exception.

Brighton's briefing, I am sure would have been to keep on top of Ivan Toney, ensure he was well marked and not to lay a hand on him in the penalty area.

None of that really happened as Ivan Toney finished one goal and then earned a penalty which he scored himself, making it Brentford 2-0 Brighton. Toney is not on Gareth Southgate's radar for the World Cup for nothing. He is the Bees main goal scorer, as important to them as Erling Haaland is for Manchester City.

It was not just Toney who the Albion had to overcome. David Raya had a blinder in goal for Brentford, proving himself to Thomas Frank after letting in five goals away at Newcastle United the previous week.

The Albion will not face two players at both ends of the pitch in such excellent form very often this season. That is a reason not to be too downhearted about the result against Brentford.

Frank must have done his homework as there was a distinct similarity between how Brentford defended against Brighton and what Tottenham had done a week earlier at the Amex.

There was no way through against Spurs and there was no way through against the Bees. Brighton tried hard and some of the opportunities should have hit the back of the net, even against a goalkeeper playing so well.

Missed chances were not the only problem. The Albion's passing has not been as slick and smooth as in previous weeks, for me.

Maybe the players are not used to being constantly shouted at from the touchline? Is adapting to Roberto De Zerbi being there rather than Graham Potter impacting concentration?

The football Brighton play is beginning to show signs of change. The back line seems much higher up the pitch and that fits in with De Zerbi's more attacking plan.

I for one am not disheartened by the results against Spurs and Brentford. We deserved more from both games, a point at the very least.

Performances have been good. Just one thing is lacking. As Warren Aspinall always says on the BBC Radio Sussex commentary team: "You have to get the ball in the onion bag, it is goals that win games."

Brighton remain in seventh place, hanging onto the tail end of the top six. After Nottingham Forest, there are some tough fixtures ahead with Chelsea at home and Manchester City away to come.

The Albion against that man Haaland. No pressure on Lewis Dunk, Joel Veltman, and Adam Webster. I am sure they can handle him. What do you think?

Sitting eighth in the Premier League is no time to panic.

Brighton 0-0 Nottingham Forest was the 100th Premier League game to be played at the Amex, as reported initially by the BBC.

A first win as head coach for Roberto De Zerbi would have been a fitting way to mark this special evening. Unfortunately, it wasn't to be as not for the first time, luck deserted the Albion in front of goal.

Celebrations were instead restricted to a pre-game light show, replacing the fireworks from recent home games. The light show was great, similar to the one at the Gtech Stadium before Brentford's 2-0 win against Brighton on Friday night.

Whoever decided to steal the box of light tricks and bring

it back from London with them deserves a pat on the back. However, we must be aware that flashing strobe lights are not suitable for all fans due to medical reasons.

To the game and wouldn't it have been great if the Albion had slotted one home in the dying minutes to shoot up to fifth in the Premier League table?

For me, our current position of eighth is still a great place to be in. Brighton's aim is to remain in the top half of the Premier League and that is exactly where we are.

As Robert Sanchez tweeted after the game to reassure fans, results are coming. I think Sanchez is dead right and we are not far away from scoring goals and winning games again.

Can anyone say hand-on-heart that the lads did not give their all and play well against Forest? They did everything apart from putting the ball in the back of the net. As the stats show.

When the teams turned around at kick-off, I felt instantly uncomfortable. There is something about kicking towards the North Stand in the first half that I don't like. Thankfully, it doesn't happen very often. Maybe I am just too superstitious!

Dean Henderson was kept on his toes throughout the game by Leandro Trossard. Henderson tipped one over and then Trossard hit the bar.

The build-up to that chance involved some short, sharp, one-touch play through midfield into the final third. It was really good to watch and showed the Albion's quality.

Solly March put a shot low to the ground just wide. Forest were blocking and defending everything but even so, at this point, you felt it was just a matter of time before a goal came from one of those chances.

Adam Webster took it upon himself to try and break the deadlock. He weaved his way up the pitch as he does so well, getting on the receiving end of a ball crossed from the right which he sent over the bar.

I wondered what De Zerbi would say during the break. More of the same was my guess as there was nothing to complain about other than the chances which had been blocked, saved or well-defended.

The second half started well with Brighton applying pressure at the South Stand goal, winning corner after corner. Danny Welbeck put a header wide after more good build-up play.

As the game wore on, I began to wonder if there might be a sting in the tail. Would Jesse Lingard suddenly spark to life? The last thing Brighton wanted or deserved would have been to lose in the last few minutes.

Forest's attempts at time-wasting towards the end became more and more obvious. I was not impressed by referee Darren England or indeed his assistants.

They let Forest get away with so much, helping them take a point. Come full time and you could see that the 0-0 draw was like a victory for the visitors.

Their chairman is similar in appearance to Demis Roussos with a beard. The reason I spotted him was that he was jumping for joy after the game as if Forest had just won the FA Cup!

I am sure the players would have felt frustrated afterwards. Personally, I think we will see these chances converted into goals in the coming games against opponents who do not want to defend all the time.

A trip to Manchester City is an interesting place to test that theory. Then a week later when Graham Potter returns to the Amex with Chelsea.

I so hope nobody gives Potter and his staff a hard time. Who would not turn down a pay increase of the one he was offered? We have to remember this is a career for these guys and often a short one at that.

There is nothing to fear from the next two games. Famous last words?

Shock sunshine in Manchester — and nearly a surprise Brighton result to match.

Saturday afternoon in late October and the sun is shining in Manchester according to BBC Radio Sussex. That came as something of a shock. If Brighton were to win away at Manchester City, it would be an even bigger surprise.

There was a reminder before kick-off at the Etihad Stadium that surprises are possible. Liverpool lost 1-0 to Nottingham Forest in the lunchtime game, the same Forest who Brighton had outplayed on Tuesday evening. Based on the performance from midweek at the Amex, I was sure the Albion could put up a great fight.

The Albion team showed no changes from the 0-0 draw with Forest. Roberto De Zerbi continues to keep faith in the same players who have drawn two and lost two so far as he still awaits his first win as Brighton manager.

Aston Villa gave us a reminder of the pressure Premier League managers are under when immediately after the defeat at Fulham on Thursday night, they sacked Steven Gerrard. The sooner De Zerbi gets that victory, the better.

The familiar sound of "Hey Jude" rang around the Etihad Stadium before kick-off, followed by "Blue Moon". Brighton were playing in their crimson away strip and made a start almost as bright as their kit, keeping City at bay for the first 10 minutes according to Johnny Cantor and Warren Aspinall.

All you could hear over the radio airwaves were Albion supporters cheering loudly. The fans were giving all they had to give, and it sounded great coming across the radio.

Danny Welbeck had a good early chance when Ederson had a howler, clearing straight to the Brighton striker. Welbeck lobbed the ball back toward the goal, but it was just off target. Another good chance had gone begging, as too many have done recently.

Aspinall pointed out that Brighton were marking City man-to-man. They were paying particularly close attention to Kevin De Bruyne and Erling Haaland, although the difficulty of the task was shown when Haaland escaped and was brought down in the box by Robert Sanchez. City's penalty appeals were rejected.

Haaland scored shortly after to make it 1-0, knocking Adam Webster out of the way in the buildup to the goal. The television commentators said it was "a little shove". I don't think so. It was more like Aspinall described it, a forearm smash that should have been a Brighton free kick preventing Haaland from netting.

City had a series of moves to try and further the lead. At one point, it sounded like they were destined to score until Lewis Dunk made a great block out for a corner.

The second City goal was nearly as questionable as the first. It arrived at 43 minutes with Haaland striking a penalty awarded when Bernardo Silva felt Pascal Gross' hands in his back and then fell over Dunk's foot.

Aspinall stated Brighton were 2-0 down at half time because of two very poor decisions. On another day, it would be Man

City 0-0 Brighton and the Albion, and De Zerbi would be praised for holding the champions for 45 minutes.

Tariq Lamptey came on at half time to see if he could make a difference. Sanchez kept Riyad Mahrez from scoring early on and then with seven minutes of the second half played, Leandro Trossard scored a blinder.

Trossard cut in down the City right and hit one that Ederson at full stretch could not get close to at his near post. When you see it on television for the first time, it comes as such a surprise to see Trossard shoot from there. No wonder Ederson was caught out.

Alexis Mac Allister next had a shot fired high over the crossbar. Great work from Mac Allister until the finish. Brighton will need to do better against Kepa Arrizabalaga next, the Chelsea goalkeeper who has looked transformed under Graham Potter.

Aymeric Laporte headed wide of Sanchez's post from a corner and so the score remained 2-1 going into the final 20 minutes.

A great Gross flick sent Trossard away moving like an express train towards Ederson. Trossard got into the City box and had Welbeck in the middle. Welbeck was waiting for the pass, but it never came, instead, Trossard shot, and Ederson made the deflection.

Then, of course, City scored to make it 3-1. De Bruyne hit a great shot with 15 minutes remaining. Brighton had done well enough and had a history of late goals to make us think they might get another one, but it did not happen this time.

The way the Albion played was a credit to them and there were a lot of social media comments afterwards from City fans saying Brighton were the best opposition that they had seen this year at the Etihad. That is a big compliment!

Now attention turns to next Saturday against Chelsea. The Albion sit ninth in the Premier League, still a good position but a win is needed soon if Brighton are to hang onto the spot in the top 10 they have occupied all season.

Who better to break the run against than Chelsea? Three points would be a spectacular result and there is no reason we cannot achieve it with the way the team played even in defeat at City. Up the Albion!

An Amex atmosphere like Brighton v Chelsea every week, please.

As we walked from the Bridge Car Park to the Amex on Saturday afternoon, my wife and I wondered how we would be feeling when making the return journey a few hours later. Grizzling thanks to Graham Potter or jumping for joy thanks to Roberto De Zerbi?

Who would have thought the Albion would come out and play so well? I did. Chelsea have been playing two games a week with their Champions League commitments and although they have been winning most recently, those exertions were bound to catch up with them at some point.

Then there was the sheer determination shown by our Brighton players. If you could bottle that and feed it to the squad before every game, we would qualify for European football easily. That desire and passion to play for the Albion is something money cannot buy — even Chelsea, with all their wealth.

Blues fans tried to claim that they played badly but nobody should buy that argument. It was the Albion playing exceptionally well which led it to finish Brighton 4-1 Chelsea.

The home support played a huge part too. The atmosphere inside the stadium felt good even before kick-off. If there was one lesson to take, it is that we must give the lads 120 percent support in every game at the Amex because it makes a massive difference.

So many games over the past couple of years that it has been left to the North Stand to chant. Us in the East Stand and those in the West should be doing just as much to generate noise, as happened against Chelsea with brilliant results.

The tone was set before the game. It seemed like everyone had taken their seats earlier than normal. Maybe this is what we need going forward — everyone in the stadium 10 minutes before kick-off to drown out the away supporters. Mind you, it only took six minutes for the players to shut up Chelsea anyway!

Much of the noise was directed at Graham Potter. I think it is important to remember how much the Albion improved under his coaching, so no matter what you might think of him now there cannot be any question that he did a lot of good during his time at Brighton.

The time for Potter to move on was always going to come.

Watching that Sky documentary in the summer showed that the writing would be on the wall sooner rather than later.

Throughout his career, Potter has taken up a new challenge once he feels he has achieved his aims. Finishing in the top 10 of the Premier League with Brighton meant his target had been reached. Potter has always switched jobs at the right time in the past, going back to even before he was managing in Sweden.

Roberto De Zerbi quite rightly said in the build-up to the game that Brighton had been playing well recently, just without the results to match. Talk about breaking that winless run of form in style.

The Albion had their first chance within a few minutes of kick-off. A bad pass by a Chelsea defender was intercepted by Pervis Estupinan and played to Leandro Trossard.

He was quite aware that Kepa Arrizabalaga was off his line and so lobbed the ball towards goal. It looked destined to go in until Thiago Silva headed over the bar whilst standing on the goal line.

The same thing happened again when Solly March's corner went from right to left and Estupinan shot, needing Silva to head it away for a second time. Four minutes played and Brighton could have been 2-0 ahead.

Marc Cucurella had his first touch of the ball shortly after. It was disappointing to hear him on the receiving end of so much booing. I can understand when someone like Kurt Zouma gets that sort of reaction for allegedly kicking a cat, but not a former "Player of the Season" who was a success story for the Albion model.

The Albion model is to buy players young, improve them and then sell them on for a profit. Brighton made £47 million on Marc Cucurella, and it is deals like that which keep the club in business. We should not forget this side of the plan when individuals move on to other clubs.

Booing for Cucurella quickly became cheers for Trossard. March worked the ball into Trossard, and a lucky bounce saw it go to Kaoru Mitoma who raced into the Chelsea area and passed three defenders.

Mitoma returned the ball to Trossard. He almost looked wrong-footed, however within a second he had worked some space and got his balance back to go around Kepa and fire into the net.

It was a great finish. De Zerbi enjoyed it, dancing on the pitch to celebrate the Albion taking the lead. I was so excited that I missed out on seeing him so excited, only catching that moment again when watching back the highlights on television.

Next March delivered a good corner from the right, where our old friend Rick O'Shea was waiting to assist the Albion with a second goal. The ball hit the leg of Ruben Loftus-Cheek and flew in, leaving Kepa with no chance.

Get in, I thought. Then I remembered who we were playing. Being 2-0 ahead with just 14 minutes played left Chelsea with a lot of time to strike back, and we know from experience that Potter's teams have a habit of scoring late goals and never knowing when they are beaten.

Conor Gallagher had a shot that required a brilliant save from Robert Sanchez, one of several he made during the game. The ball rebounded to Christian Pulisic but he could only slice wide of the Albion goal; much to his disgust. He knew it was a big chance for Chelsea and he had blown it.

Sanchez made his best stop from a Gallagher flick, springing like a cat to tip the ball over the bar. Many years ago, Chelsea goalkeeper, Peter Bonnetti used to be nicknamed the cat. I think we need to resurrect the name for Robert Sanchez if he stays at the Albion.

Moises Caicedo nearly scored with a shot that hit the post and the side netting. At that point, I felt a third goal before half time would have made life very difficult for Chelsea, but the Blues were surely not going to allow that to happen?!

A super piece of football down the left saw Moises Caicedo play a perfectly weighted pass to Pervis Estupinan. He cut inside and put in a cross which Chelsea defender Trevor Chalobah turned into his own goal before the ball could reach an Albion player.

Brighton led 3-0 going into the break and Chelsea had no idea how to cope with the Albion. I wondered what Potter would be saying to Chelsea. De Zerbi had an easier team talk surely; Brighton needed to stay psyched up and not lose concentration.

The Blues made two changes at half time, bringing on Pierre-Emerick Aubameyang and swapping goalkeepers with Kepa replaced by Edouard Mendy.

Chelsea pulled one back right at the start of the second half when Kai Havertz headed in a cross from Gallager. *Oh no, here we go,* I thought.

Sanchez made another good save, this time from Aubameyang with 20 minutes left to play. It was actually the Albion who had the better chances to win it after that point.

Substitute Julio Enciso broke away, initially on his own, and then joined by Trossard to the right. Enciso did not make the best decision, opting to shoot himself when he could have slipped the ball across to Trossard who would have had only Mendy to beat.

Enciso did better with the second chance that came his way, firing two shots in quick succession which Mendy had to block. The second rebound went to Pascal Gross, and he managed to get the ball in the back of the Chelsea goal, just onside with literally a minute to go.

There was no coming back for Chelsea now. The final whistle from referee Andy Madeley was met with an incredible roar as Roberto De Zerbi had his first win as Albion's head coach.

Now I am going to let you all into a secret. I had tears in my eyes when that whistle went. I felt so emotional, Brighton had played so well for us fans in such an important game.

They now deserve all the support we can give them in three big matches before the World Cup starts. Wolves away is followed by a Carabao Cup visit to Arsenal and then back to the Amex against Unai Emery's Aston Villa.

It is all to play for now Roberto De Zerbi is off the mark. Thank you to the Seagulls for an amazing afternoon's entertainment!

CHAPTER 4
November 2022

Brighton Dezerbed their win at Wolves as Roberto keeps rolling.

A DARK, MISERABLE, wet, and rainy day down south was made less gloomy by happenings at Molineux where Brighton made it back-to-back wins under Roberto De Zerbi for the first time... and the Albion certainly Dezerbed their three points.

The weather was not quite as bleak in the Midlands, where Johnny Cantor and Warren Aspinall both sounded in good form on BBC Radio Sussex. Both were also wearing Peaky Blinders caps in an attempt to blend in with the locals.

De Zerbi named an unchanged starting XI from last week's fantastic 4-1 win over Chelsea. You could hear the Albion fans loud and proud over the airwaves, a fantastic effort from everyone to get to Wolverhampton when there were no normal trains running. This does not deter the faithful Albion travelling fans.

It was even reported that Brighton had been given a larger away area along the side of the pitch rather than in the corner, as was the case last season. It had sold out which once again highlights what great support the players enjoy on the road.

Those at Molineux and us keeping track from elsewhere nearly had something to celebrate as early as the fourth minute. Alexis Mac Allister shot wide, followed five minutes later by Wolves defender Nathan Collins deflecting a Solly March effort behind for a corner.

March took the resulting corner, from which a series of good passes allowed Adam Lallana to slot home the opening goal.

Lallana has worked so hard for the team and shown real leadership in helping out following the departure of Graham

Potter that he deserved to score — especially having come close on so many occasions this season.

BBC Sussex informed us it was his first goal in 44 matches. What a perfect time to end such a long run without scoring, with only 10 minutes played at Molineux.

Unfortunately, the 1-0 lead did not last very long. Two minutes after Adam Lallana struck and Goncalo Guedes equalised. Guedes deserves credit for his goal; he could have gone to ground to try and earn Wolves a penalty when clipped by Kaoru Mitoma, but he stayed on his feet, getting a shot past Robert Sanchez before falling to the floor. So, it was Wolves 1 Albion 1.

Brighton responded and some good passing up the pitch gave Leandro Trossard the chance to get a shot away which flew over the crossbar.

Lallana was relatively unmarked in the middle; perhaps if Trossard had slipped a pass to his teammate then it could have been a different story with that attack.

The game went back up the other end, where Daniel Podence chipped a ball into the Brighton box from Wolves' right flank. As Lewis Dunk was about to challenge Podence, the Albion captain raised his right arm to try and balance.

As a consequence, the ball caught Dunk's elbow. Referee Graham Scott did not initially blow, however, VAR soon intervened, and we had a lengthy break in play whilst video assistant referee Lee Mason watched a thousand replays.

Eventually, Mr Scott went over to the pitch side monitor, and having looked at just one angle of the incident, he pointed to the spot straight away.

The penalty was slotted into the top of the net by Wolves top scorer Ruben Neves, putting the hosts 2-1 up. At this point, I was thinking nothing more than, *Oh no!*

Brighton though never give up. It did not take long for the Albion to equalise. March was heavily involved with some great passing and possession play, eventually leading to Lallana who crossed from the right.

The ball into the box found the head of Karou Mitoma who nodded home to make it 2-2. It was a fine header from Mitoma, the first of many goals I am sure we will see from him in a Brighton shirt. . . presuming he stays long enough!

There were six minutes of stoppage time added thanks to how long it took VAR to reach a decision on the penalty. I found myself thinking at that point that getting to half time level would be a good platform for the Albion to go on and win the game.

Those six minutes brought with them an important incident. Nelson Semedo put into practice something which he obviously learnt at Twickenham, a full-on rugby tackle of Mitoma who was racing onto a beautifully weighted long ball forward from Dunk.

Mitoma would have been in on goal had Semedo not wrapped his arms around the waste of the Albion winger and pulled him to the ground. Mr Scott showed an immediate red card with no questions asked.

There was quite a debate on BBC Sussex afterwards with some listeners telephoning in to say Mitoma should not have behaved as he did following the rugby tackle, gesticulating at the referee to show Semedo a card.

My point of view is, that Kaoru Mitoma does not yet speak English well enough, so he had every right to let Mr Scott know what he really thought by waving his arms around. The foul on Mitoma was appalling and he was quite correct to be angry.

Early in the second half and March got away down the right, hitting a really good shot that needed an impressive save from Jose Sa at the near post to stop it from going in.

There seemed to be Brighton attempt after attempt after attempt following that. Adam Webster missed a couple of headers. Danny Welbeck replaced Lallana and soon had Collins booked and a free kick was earned, which Alexis Mac Allister took. Sa made another great stop in goal.

Sanchez had to make saves from Guedes and Adama Traore as the 10 men of Wolves tried to make a fight of it. As the game entered the final 10 minutes, the score remained 2-2 with the hosts becoming more and more content to hold onto what they had.

Brighton needed to find a way through. A great passage of play in the 83rd minute got Mitoma away around the back. He flicked the ball to Deniz Undav, who laid off to Pascal Gross.

Gross swung a right leg at the ball and placed it into the right side of the Wolves net. Brighton were 3-2 ahead with just seven minutes remaining, seven minutes which they comfortably saw out for another three points.

The victory lifted Brighton into sixth in the table, above Potter, and Chelsea. It would be fantastic to go into the winter World Cup break in the top six, something the Albion will achieve with a result next week against Aston Villa.

Before that, there is the small matter of a trip to Arsenal in the League Cup. It will be interesting to see how both coaches line up their teams; but no matter how strong or weak the Gunners team is, Brighton should fear nobody at the minute as they continue rolling with Roberto De Zerbi.

Brighton make it nice being married to an Arsenal-supporting wife

Unfortunately, I was not able to be at the Emirates Stadium to watch the Albion against Arsenal in the third round of the League Cup. Instead, my Arsenal-supporting wife and I settled down to listen over the airwaves to Johnny Cantor and Warren Aspinall on BBC Radio Sussex.

When it was announced that Roberto De Zerbi had made eight changes, I was excited. It was an opportunity for the guys coming in to really shine and show what they can do.

Both benches looked strong, with Arsenal having first-choice players named as substitutes just as Brighton did. If the starting lineup found themselves in difficulty, then De Zerbi had support to call upon from the bench.

I had a great feeling about this game. The lack of television coverage highlighted how lucky we are to have Johnny, Warren, and host Adrian Harms keeping those of us who were at home up to date with all the hot news from North London.

Warren reported before kick-off that only half of the pitch was being watered. At the time, we were not aware which, if any, team may benefit.

Surely, it was all dependent on which captain won the coin toss? It seemed a strange approach to take as Arsenal could not guarantee which way they would be kicking.

The Gunners kicked things off going from left to right as Johnny and Warren saw it. I was quite amused by the commentator's comments about having their view blocked by Arsenal fans taking their seats after the game had started.

It must have been frustrating; imagine trying to do your job of telling thousands of people back in Sussex what is happening on the pitch, but you cannot see the pitch for bodies and burgers in front of you.

On the same subject, I can never really understand why people near me at the Amex arrive after the game has kicked off. Then they get up and push past after 35 minutes have gone, do not return until the 55th minute, and often leave before the final whistle blows. *What is the point?* I ask myself and then the penny drops — booze!

The 6,500 Albion supporters who had made their way to North London could be heard loud and clear over the airwaves.

If Brighton were to win, they would get to witness a bit of history — the Seagulls had never beaten Arsenal in the League Cup before. Turns out this has been quite the year for breaking records.

Neither team seemed as well-oiled as they have been in the Premier League. That was to be expected, I suppose, given all the changes both De Zerbi and Mikel Arteta had made.

There were several early chances per side. Julio Enciso for Brighton sounded as if he was determined to make his mark, being heavily involved in one of those early issues.

Arsenal took the lead in the 20th minute with a great break down the right. Watching the highlights, there appeared to be a clear foul on Jeremy Sarmiento which went completely ignored.

Reiss Nelson was able to drive forward and play the ball left to Eddie Nkeitiah, who side-footed over Jason Steele into the far post. Arsenal led 1-0 and my wife was at least happy!

Seven minutes later and I was the one cheering. A good pass from Enciso fed Solly March and he spotted the forward run of Danny Welbeck.

A perfect weighted through ball sent Welbeck away and into the box. Arsenal goalkeeper Karl Hein on his debut came out and brought down Welbeck.

Referee Jarred Gillet did not need a second to think about it, pointing to the spot. With no VAR, the referee's word was final, and Welbeck placed the ball beautifully to the right to score a great penalty.

The score remained 1-1 up to the halfway point. It sounded like Arsenal were getting closer and closer to a second after the restart, hitting the post and then drawing some great saves from Steele. Steele saves the day.

Those saves looked even more important on 58 minutes when Sarmiento carved his way through the Gunners' defence. He was not greedy, placing the ball to Kauro Mitoma who scored a great finish to make it 2-1 to the Albion.

"I told you not to gloat," said my wife. "I am not gloating, but we are definitely going to win this," I replied.

And we did win this thanks to good old Tariq Lamptey clicking on his afterburners, sprinting clear of the Arsenal defence, and slotting home to make it Arsenal 1-3 Brighton.

A fantastic game and how thrilling to see the talents of some of the players who have not had a great opportunity to play so far this season.

Confidence will be really high throughout the squad now going into the final game before the World Cup when Aston Villa and their new manager Unai Emery visit the Amex.

I am confident, at least. Are you?

How long was the ball actually in play against Aston Villa?

Lost time seems to have been a theme of this week. Before we get onto Brighton 1-2 Aston Villa, I bring you the news that this is my second attempt to offer my take on the game between Seagulls and Villans.

As I was writing the initial piece on Monday evening, I leant across the table at home to reach for something. Whilst doing this, I must have caught the Samsung keyboard and the screen went white. Shock, horror, panic, where are those two pages I have just written?

Surely, I thought not gone for good? I thought the article was pretty good, one of my better efforts. I had so much to tell you all.

I went digging around in Google Docs, temporary files, and even on the web as well. However, it was all in vain. Nothing could be recovered from either my Android device or the internet and so it was back to the drawing board.

It seemed apt that this happened whilst writing about the visit of Aston Villa. Like my Samsung losing two hours work, Villa were also masters at time wasting which made for a frustrating afternoon at the Amex.

At least there could be no complaints about the weather. It was a beautiful Sunday at the Amex. The skies were blue, the poppies for Remembrance Sunday were red and to go with their timewasting Villa picked up enough yellow cards to make the pitch look as if it were a buttercup field. And of course, Roberto De Zerbi was booked on the touchline.

Villa have a new head of their family in Unai Emery and they were benefitting from the new manager bounce having beaten Manchester United 3-1 a week earlier.

Even though Brighton were buzzing off the back of winning 3-1 at Arsenal on Wednesday night, the Emery factor gave this the look of a tough game. The impression I got from others I chatted to was that most of us expected an Albion victory though.

I was standing outside the Amex Superstore at 10.40 a.m. — yes that early — waiting to repurchase an Albion Poppy Pin that my dear neighbour had bought for me, and which had dropped off my jacket walking between the Bridge Car Park and Falmer Station.

So, if you happened to find such a pin on the path it was mine. Whilst waiting for the shop to open, the wonderful waft of fish and chips and the smell of burgers came flowing across the ticket office area.

There were some musicians warming up and the brass instruments were heard practicing Good Old Sussex by The Sea.

Things felt good and my reason for arriving so early was that I had been given special permission by Mr Paul Camlin who is head of media and communications to learn from Johnny Cantor what goes on in the commentary box. But more on that later, presuming the Samsung device does not suffer a funny turn once again.

The visit of Aston Villa was of course our last game in the Premier League before the World Cup of 2023. It will be six weeks then through until Boxing Day when Albion make the trip to Southampton when the Premier League fully resumes.

Then on New Year's Eve, it is back to the Amex where we will face Arsenal again. Oh God, I must keep my head down with my wife's family supporting the Gunners and our win at the Emirates is still fresh in the mind.

Speaking of the World Cup, it's amazing that eight Albion players will be representing their countries. Moises Caicedo, Pervis Estupinan, and Jeremy Sarmiento are all headed to Qatar with Ecuador.

We have Alexis Mac Allister playing for Argentina and slipping passes through to Lionel Messi, I am sure. Kauro Mitoma is with the Japanese squad and Tariq Lamptey representing Ghana.

Two of our Europeans are there too; Robert Sanchez with Spain and of course the man-of-the-moment Leandro Trossard hoping to make an impression for Belgium.

It will be warm in Qatar, and it was warm at the Amex too; so warm I had to remove my coat. Two local Salvation Army offices Mr Crombie and Mr Warren played the Last Post on their bugles before kick-off. De Zerbi and Emery both laid wreaths at the side of the touchline to remember the fallen in battle.

A different type of battle then took place, and it did not take long for Brighton to gain an advantage. Adam Lallana kicked off back to Robert Sanchez, followed by the Albion moving down the left-hand side.

The ball went out for a throw which Villa worked back to Emiliano Martinez. Then Adam Lallana was so clever in what he did next, initially running towards Tyrone Mings on the right.

Lallana then swung across at speed directly towards Martinez. The pass to Mings was cut out and so Martinez having taken too much time now had no option but to play the ball to Douglas Luiz who was facing the Villa goal.

Little did Luiz know that Mac Allister was on his back. Luiz went to ground as Mac Allister stole the ball before firing off a shot that went straight in. 1-0 to the Albion in 58 seconds thanks to some great thinking by Adam Lallana.

Brighton had to produce some excellent defending after that up until the 19th minute when Villa equalised. A break by John McGinn allowed him to get through the middle and although Lewis Dunk did his best to challenge McGinn, the Albion captain clipped the Villa midfielder who went down in the area.

Referee Chris Kavanagh did not hesitate, immediately blowing for a penalty. Danny Ings eventually stepped up to the plate.

Robert Sanchez is yet to save a Premier League penalty and although he got his left hand onto the ball, the power of the shot was so great he was not able to keep it out.

Brighton came back with a couple of corners as they attempted to reestablish themselves. There were few chances though and the sides went into the break level at 1-1. Oh, to be a fly on the wall to hear De Zerbi's advice to the team.

The second half began with a very near miss early on from Aston Villa. Matty Cash crossed to the head of Emiliano Buendia whose effort hit Robert Sanchez's right post and went out towards the East Stand.

Solly March had the ball but nowhere to go other than back to Joel Veltman. Veltman passed to Mac Allister who lost possession, leaving Ings to hit a weak shot that beat all of Dunk, Levi Colwill, and Sanchez.

It seemed a weird goal to concede as the speed of the ball was so slow and it crept in at the near post. Brighton now had it all to do in the remaining 36 minutes.

Their task was made very difficult by how scrappy things became, largely through Villa's time-wasting. I could not believe how many times Martinez — a goalkeeper I have really admired in the past for his skill — could be so unprofessional with all his playacting and wasting of time.

Villa ending up with seven yellow cards was telling. Roberto De Zerbi also had his name taken by Mr Kavanagh the referee, following the game in a press conference he stated he used to think the Premier League was a fair arena to play in. I bet he was having second thoughts on that after Brighton 1-2 Aston Villa!

I would love to know how much time the ball was actually in play. A long way short of the 90 minutes a game of football is supposed to last would be my guess, robbing the Albion of the chance to get back into the tie.

Still, it is not all bad news. Brighton will sit seventh in the table on Christmas Day with a points tally of 21, and above Chelsea on goal difference.

Let us hope that the success can continue after the World Cup and that De Zerbi delivers an even greater 2023 than 2022 has been.

A Day in the Life of the Albion BBC Radio Sussex Commentary Team

Sunday, November 13th, 2022. The World Cup where so many Brighton players would showcase their talents in front of a worldwide audience of billions was yet to start.

The sun was beaming down on the Amex Stadium. It was too warm even to wear a jacket. And I found myself joining the BBC

Radio Sussex Commentary team as the Albion took on Aston Villa in their final Premier League game before the winter break.

It was listening to Brighton playing an away game on BBC Radio Sussex that the idea came to me. How many of us appreciate the effort that goes into bringing commentary and coverage over the airwaves to the Albion fans come rain, shine, sleet, and on occasion, snow?

At this summer's Albion Fans' Forum, I approached the host Mr Johnny Cantor. He very kindly helped publicise my book *The Seagulls Best Ever Season* on the "Albion Unlimited Podcast", and so I asked him if he and his co-commentator Mr Warren Aspinall would mind if I became a fly-on-the-wall watching, understanding, and getting the inside line on what goes on in their commentary position at the Amex?

Johnny agreed and so too did the head of communications at Brighton, Mr Paul Camilin. It was decided that I would join BBC Radio Sussex for the Villa game; a choice I was very happy with as maybe the now-new Prince of Wales would be there.

He is an avid Villa fan as we all know. Unfortunately, I did not spot him that day but that does that mean he was not present, incognito does it. If William were at the Amex, he would have left a happy man afterwards. Villa won 2-1, a blow to Roberto De Zerbi and Brighton as they had been on a good run beforehand.

Sixth place going into that Villa game became seventh place after, still it was a great position to be in ahead of the six-week break for the World Cup.

Joining Johnny and Warren was not my first experience of sports commentary. Many of my early years were spent in the golf business and I was a regular visitor to the trade exhibitions, working for both Golf Illustrated and Golf Monthly magazines.

One exhibition was a trade fair in Edinburgh on a cold January. Mr Renton Laidlaw, the then-ITV golf commentator, had a competition running at the show.

To win the prize, you had to commentate on the famous Seve Ballesteros playing an approach shot to a green at Wentworth.

I knew Wentworth well, having played the course before and so commentating on it was for me, as the meerkats say, "Simples." And the first prize became mine.

Johnny and Warren have a far more difficult job to do when

it comes to commentating on the Albion. There is no warm commentary box. They sit out in the open at every game, often in not-the-best of conditions.

Commentary teams from BBC local radio have no engineers or technicians with them; they do everything themselves.

There is a lengthy setup requiring an early arrival to make sure all the equipment is working. It then all must be packed away afterwards, followed by the long drive home if the game has taken place up north. Matchday for Johnny and Warren is more time-consuming than you would ever realise.

Johnny is no stranger to it. He is a hugely experienced broadcaster both on the radio and television he has covered sports, news as well as entertainment.

His voice and commentaries are familiar to thousands of people in Sussex and also nationally having been heard on BBC programmes such as *Football Focus* and *Late Kick Off*, and BBC Radio 5 Live's Monday Night Club.

Johnny has presented from some of the most famous sporting venues in the world. Wembley, Lords, Wimbledon, Epsom Racecourse, and even the golf course which won my commentary prize all those years ago, Wentworth.

He is a regular host of award ceremonies and fans' forums, he also lectures at universities, does voiceovers for commercials including the *Radio Times* magazine, and has even worked as a researcher for the investigative show "Inside Out" on football finances.

To watch and learn from Johnny is to watch and learn from a broadcaster who has done it all. On the day of the Villa game, I arrived at the Amex before 11 a.m.

After hearing some musicians playing "Sussex by the Sea" near the fish and chip stand in the sunshine and smelling a waft of burgers and chips, everything seemed set for a great afternoon.

I met up with Johnny at the Amex Press Centre and after observing the two-minute silence for Remembrance Sunday in honour of all those who made the ultimate sacrifice, it was down to business. Warren would join us shortly but there was no Mr Adrian Harmes as he was on holiday in Egypt. Alright for some!

With three hours until kick-off, the press centre was already a hive of activity. Broadcasters and journalists from local, national, and international media were all at their desks and working away.

There had been a significant increase in interest surrounding Brighton since Roberto De Zerbi had been appointed, whilst Villa were also attracting attention as Unai Emery took charge of his first away game for Aston Villa. This was reflected by every desk being full that day.

Many had been at the Amex since the early hours and would remain in place long after the stadium had emptied, working through the afternoon and beyond to reach their deadlines. With commuting to and from the stadium, those working in the media face a very long day.

From the press centre refreshment area came the scent of chicken curry. There was the regular sound of fizzy drink bottles being opened and consumed by hard-working journalists.

The Albion's hospitality team do an important job of making sure the media are fed and watered before kick-off. With those tight deadlines to meet, broadcasters and journalists often face a lengthy wait to eat again after the final whistle.

Warren and Johnny know only too well from their experience at away games the importance of sustenance. Many of the people in the press centre will have faced long journeys to the Amex. A good meal on arrival is a welcome sight after hours on the road.

Johnny explained that the BBC would have three teams at the match. His counterparts from BBC West Midlands who were providing coverage for Villa fans back in Birmingham and BBC Radio 5 Live were also present that day as the game had been selected as the day's afternoon commentary on the station.

Right on cue, in walked Mr Glenn Murray. The former Brighton striker has now made a name for himself as a pundit since retiring, although to me he remains the Albion's second-highest-ever goal scorer and an absolute hero of mine.

To be so close to Murray, well, it was hard to concentrate on what Johnny was saying for a minute. The spell was broken when Johnny took me outside to the BBC Sussex commentary position overlooking the Albion turf.

It is in a prime spot, right behind the dugouts, so prime that it became the centre of attention during one of the greatest afternoons in Albion history.

When Brighton beat Wigan Athletic to secure promotion to the Premier League on Monday 17th April 2017, the players celebrated from where Johnny and Warren sit and broadcast from.

Cue Johnny, he was caught in one of the best photos of that great day, looking up from just behind Anthony Knockaert as Knockaert and Bruno sang to fans who had invaded the pitch.

Despite everything going on around him, Johnny was still broadcasting away in the thick of it all to keep those at home up to date with the celebrations taking place.

Back to the business of the day and whilst Johnny untangled his wires and set up the commentary position for Warren and himself, the BBC West Midlands team did likewise one desk along.

Johnny whipped out the box of tricks which brings his voice and that of Warren to us over the airwaves. It is all run through an ISDN line provided by the Albion.

ISDN lines have been around for many years, they even kept my telex machine running many moons ago. Some broadcasters have switched to Hi-Speed Broadband and Wi-Fi, but not all. For BBC Radio Sussex, ISDN remains the way at present in which they connect with their audience at this time.

As Johnny was sorting out the technical side of things, Warren remained inside. He was busy making notes and going over any information that may be needed during the broadcast, as well as practicing singing "What Did Della Wear Boys, What Did Della Wear?" Warren had also broadcast a rendition of this song over the air the week before during the 5 p.m. Final Whistle programme.

Not many people can say they have been serenaded by a former Brighton striker performing a 1950s classic. My day with the BBC Sussex team was already proving better than expected.

Warren went back to his notes once he had finished performing. The level of detail and preparation put in by both Johnny and Warren is amazing.

It even went down to the name of the Salvation Army buglers who would be playing the Last Post on the pitch before the game.

Although there was not enough room for me to remain with Johnny and Warren during the whole game, I was lucky enough to sit with Johnny whilst he gave the 1 p.m. announcement of the teams live on air on BBC Radio Sussex.

With the headphones on, I became even more excited than when Warren had been singing for me. To think that there were tens of thousands of people across Sussex and beyond finding out that Adam Webster and Kaoru Mitoma were both ill and that Levi Colwill was making his Premier League debut, highlighted what an important role BBC Sussex plays for Albion fans.

How many of us would miss the service if it were taken away? Imagine no more Johnny, Warren, and Adrian bringing us live commentaries of every Brighton match. No more interviews with De Zerbi or the players. No more Albion Unlimited.

The reason I mention this is because many broadcasters currently working in BBC local radio all over the UK faced the possibility of losing their jobs in the new year of 2023.

According to reports in the media, nobody is safe. The *Hull Daily Mail* revealed in November 2022 that their region faced major cuts to jobs and local programming.

The *Manchester Evening News* followed up the story by reporting presenters have been told to reapply for their jobs amid plans to slash staff.

Industry website Radio Today said every local BBC reporter had been told they face the risk of redundancy.

The loss to Albion fans and radio listeners in Sussex would be massive, if Johnny, Warren, Adrian, and the rest of their colleagues were to be taken off air.

It could also lead to no more matchday commentary via the official club website, as that too is supplied by BBC Radio Sussex.

It has never been more important to support our local radio station than now by listening in. Brighton fans need to leave the BBC in no doubt that we do not want them to remove the first-rate coverage of the Seagulls we are treated to when these decisions set to be in the Spring get made.

BBC Radio Sussex provides Brighton coverage that we don't get anywhere else. Thanks to Johnny and Warren for allowing me to join them, I saw firsthand the hard work, commitment, and dedication they put into the job.

We cannot let that disappear, because without Johnny, who would keep us up to date on games from Manchester City to Forest Green Rovers or tell us "It's the stuff of champions, it's the stuff of dreams"?

And without Warren, who would talk about putting the ball in the onion bag or sing over the airwaves "What Did Della Wear Boys, What Did Della Wear?"

Long live BBC Radio Sussex.

CHAPTER 5
December 2022

Write off Charlton as warm up for the Premier League return.

FROM WATCHING FOOTBALL coming from the warm, dark evenings of Qatar to the damp and drizzle of South London on a dismal December night. Charlton away in the League Cup was quite a culture shock for both Brighton players and supporters.

We had all been waiting for the Albion to return to action; however, the final result at the Valley did not go in our favour.

To be beaten in sudden death of a penalty shootout and miss out on a chance to go through to the quarter-finals of the League Cup for only the second time in Albion history was disappointing, but was it really surprising?

Regular Brighton supporters know that the Albion do not do things the easy way. Strange and shock results like this have gone both for us in the past as well as against us.

Charlton have played throughout the World Cup with League One receiving no winter break. They had a match sharpness Brighton did not, in what was really a final warm-up match before the Premier League returns on Boxing Day.

If losing to Charlton means the players are better prepared and sharper at Southampton, then that seems like a good thing. It is the Premier League that matters most, would you agree?

Southampton might even be lured into overconfidence if they listened to BBC Radio Sussex and heard Johnny Cantor and Warren Aspinall's commentary of the game. They both seemed frustrated.

I was listening as I could not go to Charlton. If I had, then it appears the ticket situation would have meant queuing to collect outside the Valley because of the number of duplicate tickets needing to be distributed due to the Royal Mail strike!

Brighton had more than 6000 fans at Charlton and had taken over the area around the commentary position, leaving Johnny and Warren in the middle of the Albion support.

It could be clearly heard over the airwaves what they thought of referee Thomas Bramall's decisions to dismiss two Albion calls for penalties. There was no VAR to check, and commentary told us Mr Bramall was not even giving a fair decision on the issues.

We all know that from time to time, a game comes along where we get none of the decisions going our way because of referees not wanting to enforce the rules.

Emiliano Martinez got away with constant time-wasting when we lost to Aston Villa in November. He was booked in the World Cup final because of a stronger referee.

There appeared to be a lot of time-wasting going on from Charlton, which they were allowed to get away with like Martinez. It sounded like they were playing for a draw right from the start to take their chance on penalties.

Johnny and Warren informed us before kick-off that Charlton had not won in League One for eight games. That explains their approach but also sounded like a kiss of death for the Albion!

Charlton number 33 Miles Leasburn had the home side's first chance at the far post when he tried to beat Jason Steele but without success.

Lewis Dunk had a header fairly early which missed the target. Brighton were soon into their stride, playing some of the lovely passing football we have come to expect.

Tariq Lamptey turned and poked right to play a one-two with Solly March. Lamptey streaked away and made an early cross which got to Adam Lallana, weaving a little to hit a shot from the edge of the penalty area which clipped the top of the bar.

Steve Sessegnon sounded prominent for Charlton but thankfully the chances he had did not pass either Dunk or Steele. It was 0-0 at the break with Warren saying the Albion's general play was too narrow and also too slow.

The second half brought an early penalty shout from Deniz Undav which was not given. Brighton did not get any luck after that as great attempts from March, Levi Colwill, and Leandro Trossard were missed.

There were several great crosses put across the Charlton goal but no Albion player was available to get the touch needed to turn them into the net.

Kaoru Mitoma came on and tried to weave some magic without much success. A second penalty appeal was waved away when Pervis Estupinan went down in the box.

Johnny and Warren thought Jesurun Rak-Sakyi had chopped Estupinan's legs away and it sounded like the Albion fans around the commentary position agreed.

When the full-time whistle blew on Charlton 0-0 Brighton, it was straight to penalties. Brighton won the toss which meant Pascal Gross took the first kick in front of the Albion supporters.

Gross missed by hitting the left post. Jayden Stockley for Charlton then hit the right post. Next came Trossard who hit the right side of the bar.

Former Albion player Jake Forster-Caskey became the first player to score, giving Charlton a 1-0 lead after two penalties each.

Evan Ferguson got Brighton off the mark, so we have a 1-1 situation. Steele saved from George Dobson with a great stop to his left.

Dunk made it 2-1 and when Steele made another brilliant save from Rak-Sakyi, March had the chance to win it. He stepped up and did a Harry Kane, skying the ball miles over the bar.

Corey Blackett-Taylor beat Steele to make it 2-2. Lamptey scored and Brighton led 3-2. Sessegnon continued his fine 90 minutes by converting his penalty by sending Steele the wrong way.

At 3-3, Moises Caicedo missed. With the shootout in sudden death, Samuel Lavelle scored to send Charlton into the quarter-finals 4-3 on penalties.

Roberto De Zerbi apologised for the Albion's elimination afterwards and I am sure the result gave him and the squad plenty of food for thought.

Penalties look like an area they need to work on, not just for this type of knockout game but in the Premier League too. With Alexis Mac Allister not around, who of our experienced players would you back to score when the pressure is on?

Brighton though could be excused for their rustiness in a first competitive game for nearly five weeks. It was almost like a pre-season friendly for the Albion against opponents who have been playing twice a week through November and December.

With a busy holiday period coming up, it is better to use the League Cup to get rid of the cobwebs than Southampton in the main business of the Premier League.

Had the Albion played Charlton immediately after the Villa and Arsenal games back in November, the momentum would probably have seen us win at the Valley.

We support the squad through the good and the bad. What is needed now is plenty of PMA — yes, "positive mental attitude". That goes for the players as well as the fans.

Stuffed turkey and stuffed Saints makes a good Christmas

The World Cup has come and gone along with Christmas as well, which meant Boxing Day was upon us and the restart of the Premier League.

Things got off to an exciting start with the lunchtime game featuring Brentford at home to Spurs. Brentford went 2-0 up but left the door open for Spurs to equalise as they finished with a point apiece.

The result kept the Albion seventh in the table ahead of our own Boxing Day trip to Southampton, where the sun was shining, the sky was blue and conditions were good for football.

Amazon Prime were showing every game in this round of Premier League matches. I have their service for business reasons but still stuck with Johnny Cantor and Warren Aspinall on BBC Radio Sussex at the same time. This ensured I knew immediately what was happening at the match without the 30-second delay.

Southampton had only won six points at home this season, but Brighton did not have a particularly good record against the Saints.

Albion fans were singing their hearts out as our squad walked onto the St Mary's Stadium turf, they were heard loud and proud over the radio airwaves.

Applause for the late George Cohen who had passed away recently was played out by all the players and the fans before the kick-off. Cohen's passing leaves only Sir Bobby Charlton and Sir Geoff Hurst still alive from the 1966 World Cup-winning team.

Southampton started the game looking more likely to take an early lead. Then as if by magic, the inference swung Albion's way with Brighton playing the most delightful football.

Brighton began to be quicker on the ball than Southampton, and the passing was so exact the stats said it all. One of the Amazon Prime commentators said, and I quote: "If you put light blue shirts on the Albion players, you would think you are watching Manchester City." What a compliment that was!

The stats showed we had 66 percent possession overall in the game and 680 passes to Southampton's 329. Our passing accuracy was shown as 86.8 percent.

This football was what Roberto De Zerbi wants from his players. If it continues, it will begin to raise eyebrows across the Premier League, and it certainly has done that as we all now know.

It was truly amazing. There was so much energy chasing and winning second balls and the goals stemmed from great play up and down the lines.

We first saw how important wide play would be when Kaoru Mitoma's magic nearly got us the first goal. It needed a good save by the Southampton goalkeeper Gavin Bazunu.

Then came the opener for the Albion. Great build-up from Adam Lallana playing the ball out wide to the right to Solly March, who returned the ball towards the penalty spot.

Lallana got an important touch on the header and placed the ball to Bazunu's right to put Brighton into the lead. What a gracious man Lallana was, no heavy celebrations as he respected his old club.

Southampton teased a free kick in a dangerous position for James Ward-Prowse to take right in the area where he is normally lethal.

Thankfully, the free kick went a foot wide of Robert Sanchez's right-hand post. Sanchez still made an amazing cat-like dive which meant that had Ward-Prowse's shot been on target, Sanchez would have actually probably saved it.

The next impressive piece of play by the Albion saw build-up down the left side which sent Mitoma away like the Tokyo to Yokohama Express Bullet Train.

Mitoma was closely chased by Estupinan, who overtook Mitoma to receive a pass on the overlap. Estupinan crossed towards goal with March charging to the back post, where the ball dropped at the feet of Southampton defender Romain Perraud to deflect nicely into his own net.

Brighton led 2-0 but there was no let up. More link up and

down the left saw Leandro Trossard racing away and crossing for Mitoma whose header went over the bar.

Next, Mitoma put a great cross into the box which March could not get a foot on. Brighton could have easily led by four or five going into the break, so whilst 2-0 was a good scoreline you also felt the game could have already been put to bed.

Southampton made some changes for the second half and youngster Samuel Edozie had a really good early chance. Luckily for Brighton, he did a Harry Kane and sent the ball over the stand and nearly into the water surrounding Southampton's harbour.

It was down to March to show Edozie how to do it. March hit a blinder of a shot from outside the penalty area which found its way into the top left-hand corner of the net like a rocket.

It was a strike on par with World Cup winner Alexis Mac Allister at the Amex against Leicester City earlier in the season.

Bazunu had no chance with the goal underlying the potential March has. He has already improved under the new coaching team, and I cannot wait to see how De Zerbi gets even more out of him over the coming years.

Solly March was having one of his best games of the season. Next, he teased Kyle Walker-Peters before putting a pass across the Saints goal. Mitoma just needed a touch with the goal gaping, but he could not connect accurately and put the header wider.

Edozie broke up the other end, beating Moises Caicdeo and Joel Veltman but running straight into Pascal Gross. It was like Edozie had hit a brick wall he had not spotted and even though the Southampton player should have shown greater awareness of Pascal Gross, referee Robert Jones had no hesitation in awarding a penalty.

Sanchez was not impressed and received a yellow card for his troubles in confronting the ref. Ward-Prowse stepped up to take the penalty; as he did, I was saying to myself that Sanchez was going to save it.

Well, initially he made a great save. But the ball bounced straight back from his hands and was headed back into the net by Ward-Prowse to make it Southampton 1-3 Brighton.

The 73rd minute brought Sanchez into focus again. Che Adams fouled Levi Colwill on the edge of the Brighton box, continuing his run and running through to blatantly charge into Sanchez.

Sanchez lost his temper and confronted Adams. Hurriedly, Lewis Dunk separated the pair, doing his captain's job. Luckily, nothing further occurred. It was a stupid move on the part of Adams; there was no need to go into Sanchez and cause such problems.

As Mr Jones blew the full-time whistle, the sound of booing could be heard around St Mary's with Southampton fans far from happy with their new team and manager Nathan Jones.

It was only a few years back that Jones managed the Albion at the Amex in a Boxing Day game. Now, he was on the end of a defeat against Brighton on Boxing Day. How things change.

This was another good three points for Brighton to add to their points tally with Southampton stuffed like the Christmas turkey we had a day earlier.

Next up, it is the Gunners on New Year's Eve. I will again find myself keeping quiet as my wife's side of the family are lifelong Arsenal fans.

PMA — a "positive mental attitude" — can see us through. Thanks to the Albion for the great Christmas gift and here is hoping for another present to kick off 2023 with.

Positives to take as Premier League leaders worried by Brighton.

After an age away from the Amex, New Year's Eve and the visit of Premier League leaders Arsenal finally arrived.

The Albion welcomed everyone back with pyrotechnics and a light show before kick-off whilst American Express kindly offered all fans a season 10 percent discount on food and drink inside the ground. A nice gesture that they did not have to do.

There were two wonderful tributes paid before the game, one to the King of Football Pele. The other was to lifelong Brighton fan Mr Ken Valder, who was born in 1955 and sadly passed away recently.

Mr Valder was named Brighton Fan of the Year for the 2017-18 season, and he seemed to reach people beyond football.

The programme carried a lovely article about Mr Valder on page 12 of that games programme. It certainly brings the reality home, as I was also born that year and sometimes wonder to myself how many more times, I will get to see the lads play. RIP to both Pele and Mr Valder.

Some readers may know that in my household, the other side of the family are born and bred Arsenal supporters from North London.

So, this fixture is always challenging, and lots of banter starts in the build-up to the game. You can probably imagine that I have enjoyed recent matches, both in the Premier League and the Carabao Cup at the Emirates just before the World Cup break.

With Arsenal top of the table, I was expecting some sort of comeback from the Gunners on this occasion. Steadying myself for the worst would mean that I avoided being too disappointed if we did lose.

An already tough task looked even harder with the players Brighton would be missing. Moises Caicedo suspended, Alexis Mac Allister still in Argentina, and defensive stalwart Adam Webster and creative forward Danny Welbeck both injured made me fear the Albion would be toppled on the day.

The inclement rain eased up as we approached the Amex, but the wind remained. It made passing challenging during the game, yet this was an area where Brighton outshone Arsenal with a passing accuracy of 88.3 percent compared to 72.6 percent.

Referee Anthony Taylor blew his whistle to start the game and instantly the Gunners looked dangerous. Arsenal captain Martin Odegaard raced from the right side towards the Brighton goal and I thought to myself this was not good.

No matter, Tariq Lamptey made an excellent interception and began racing forward. But having gained possession, Lamptey had the ball swiftly taken from him.

Oleksandr Zinchenko passed to Gabriel Martinelli who crossed. There was a slight deflection off Levi Colwill into the path of Bukayo Saka who let it drop and swept the ball beyond Robert Sanchez.

Not a great start to the evening and Sanchez was clearly unhappy, gesticulating to either the referee or his defence about what had just happened.

In celebrating their goal, Arsenal employed a timewasting tactic on par with the unfairness displayed by Emiliano Martinez when Brighton were beaten by Aston Villa last time at the Amex.

Every Gunners player met up in the corner, stayed in a little huddle for a long time, and then dawdled back to the centre circle with Eddie Nkeitah being the worst offender.

Arsenal would soon sharpen up if a rule was introduced saying that the conceding team could restart the game as soon as they were ready, and the referee blew his whistle.

Such a law change would stop these silly schoolboy antics of wasting time. What do you think? Arsenal after all did not employ the slow celebration once, but every time they scored.

Something needs to be done. Brighton do not behave like that when they score; celebrate, yes, but not for 10 minutes.

Sanchez's mood was not improved when Arsenal had another opportunity shortly after the game finally restarted.

Zincehnko crept in and it needed a good save from the Albion's number one to prevent the Gunners from doubling their lead. The highlights showed Sanchez's facial expression as not happy as the chance should not have been able to happen.

Lamptey made a run down the right without being tackled this time and crossed towards Adam Lallana on the edge of the box.

Lallana teed up Leandro Trossard, who despite a slight mishit was not far wide of the post. It certainly gave Aaron Ramsdale something to think about.

Arsenal produced some nice passing next in the Brighton penalty box. Odegaard's little flick went through the legs of Lewis Dunk to drop for Martinelli.

Martinelli tried to square but Colwill did really well to not only clear the ball away from danger but get it to Kaoru Mitoma on the left wing.

That started a fantastic passage of play from the Albion. Mitoma found Gross who released Pervis Estupinan to produce an immaculate switch from left to right to Trossard.

Next, the ball was played down the line to Solly March. He beat Zinchenko and squared across goal, only for there to be no Brighton player available to pop it into the back of the net.

Arsenal could not clear, and the ball came back out only as far as Pascal Gross. He squared to Trossard whose shot needed Ramsdale to tip it over the crossbar.

After all that excitement, Brighton conceded a second goal with six minutes until half time. Saka took a corner headed away by Billy Gilmour to the feet of Odegaard and he fired the bouncing ball off the turf, spinning it into the top right corner.

Having watched the first half from the East Upper, I had not been that impressed by the Albion. Watching the highlights back, however, the Albion looked much better from the perspective of watching on television.

You could understand why Roberto De Zerbi felt Arsenal had been lucky as they had scored from two fortunate situations.

And at least we had not scored two own goals like poor Leicester City defender Wout Faes, whose unwanted double sent the Foxes to a 2-1 defeat against Liverpool.

What advice did De Zerbi give at half time, we wonder? Certainly not to concede a third two minutes after kick-off, which transpired when Sanchez spilt a shot to Nkeita who scored a poacher's finish.

Sanchez next saved from point-blank range to ensure it did not become 4-0. After that, Brighton came into the game and finished much the stronger side. You could even say we De Zerbi-ed something from the match.

Gilmour played a ball through to Gross who rolled it into Mitoma. That fine approach play left Mitoma with a chance to shoot and he calmly beat Ramsdale to make it Brighton 1-3 Arsenal.

There was no hanging about from Mitoma, who collected the ball out the net and jogged at pace back to the centre circle, ready to go in hunt of another.

Jeremy Sarmiento put a great ball across the box but there was no striker there to convert. From there, Brighton were caught on the counter with Odegaard sweeping a magical pass out to Martinelli.

That sparked a footrace between Martinelli and Lamptey. Both were going at full throttle but Lamptey could just not catch him.

Once Martinelli made it into the box, he got a shot away. Sanchez managed to get a foot to it but the ball went straight in to give Arsenal a fourth.

More time-wasting followed and that really should have been game over. Brighton though never give up until the fat Italian lady sings. That is the saying, right?

In the remaining 13 minutes plus added time, the Albion made a real mark. Dunk hit a long ball over the top for substitute Evan Ferguson.

It dropped perfectly for Ferguson, using his body weight to beat William Saliba and finish past Ramsdale.

With the scoreline reading Brighton 2-4 Arsenal, things were getting interesting. Arsenal players and fans were suddenly a little concerned.

The Albion hammered away at Arsenal right up until a key point in the game arrived on 88 minutes. Gross took a throw that found Mitoma who scored again.

There seemed to be nothing wrong with the goal, but VAR looked and found a Mitoma bootlace offside. It was extremely unfair on the Albion, especially when Mr Taylor added on seven minutes.

Had Mitoma's goal stood, then Brighton were so on top that it is fair to assume they would have managed a draw. What a comeback that would have been.

To give the Premier League leaders so much to worry about was a thoroughly positive way to end what has been a memorable 2022. Play like that throughout 2023 and it will be another year in which Brighton shine in the Premier League.

CHAPTER 6
January 2023

The sound of home fans booing is music to Brighton ears.

ON A DARK, dingy January day when the rain poured, we were all hoping that the Albion could bring some light into the evening by seeing off Everton at Goodison Park.

They certainly did that, winning 4-1 on what proved to be a very sticky night for the Toffees when you needed a Mackintosh to keep dry.

Brighton were amazing and not for the first time, the lads produced a performance on the road resulting in the home team being booed off the pitch.

I have lost count of the number of occasions this has happened now, but whenever it does it is music to Brighton ears and a real complement to our club.

Everton fans had been very vocal in their criticism of their side last time Brighton went to Goodison, winning 3-2 last January.

Rafa Benitez had been in charge then and although they have since changed manager and put Frank Lampard in charge, the same problems continue which the Albion were able to take advantage of.

There were four changes to the Brighton side from the defeat to Arsenal. Evan Ferguson made his first Premier League start after scoring from the bench at home on New Year's Eve.

Ferguson is showing tremendous potential at just 18 years of age; as one fan put it on social media, is he our new Glenn Murray?

Joel Veltman was back in the XI alongside Moises Caicedo after his one-match ban for five yellow cards with Jeremy Sarmiento coming in for his first Premier League start of the season.

Also of note was World Cup hero Alexis Mac Allister being back on the bench as part of his gentle reintroduction to the side.

I bet he found the pouring rain and howling wind of Liverpool a little different from four weeks in Qatar followed by all those celebrations in sunny Argentina. Welcome back, Alexis!

Our trusted BBC Radio Sussex commentary team of Johnny Cantor and Warren Aspinall had navigated the motorway system to reach the northwest with the bad weather following them all the way from Sussex.

Listening to Johnny and Warren describing their seated position at Goodison is a reminder that being a commentator can be a challenging task.

They were squashed into a tiny space so cramped that neither could feel anything below their knees — although Warren did admit that this may have been because he had put on more weight at Christmas than first thought.

Radio commentators will be looking forward to Everton's new £500 million stadium at the Docklands which the Toffees hope to occupy for the 2024-25 season. Will it open in the Premier League or the Championship for them?

Brighton took to the turf in their bright crimson kit as the usual Everton theme of Z Cars played over the airwaves.

The Toffees were kicking towards the famous Gladys Street End, bringing back memories for Aspinall who played as a striker for Everton many years ago.

I listened intently as our commentators told us Everton looked really up for it, winning all the early 50/50 challenges.

The Toffees should have taken the lead when a Demari Gray free kick was floated over the Albion defence to Dominic Calvert-Lewin.

He found Alex Iwobi, who let rip with a shot beautifully saved by Robert Sanchez just getting his left hand to the ball and putting it beyond the far post.

Brighton came into the game after that. Solly March broke down the right, easily beat Vitalii Mykolenko, and crossed to the middle for Kaoru Mitoma to put a header over the bar.

Mitoma should have done better with the chance. All was forgiven not long after, however. Caicedo played a great ball to the left to find Mitoma.

He snaked his way into the penalty area, carried out a lovely swivel, and slotted past Jordan Pickford to give the Albion a 14th-minute lead.

I was up and out of my seat, meaning the settee springs are starting to suffer once again. Little could I have predicted they would be hammered three further times over the next hour.

If Brighton keep scoring goals at their current rate under Roberto De Zerbi, I am going to need a whole new sofa by the time the season is out.

March went on another good run from the Albion box, slipping a pass to Caicedo who accelerated away. Caicedo found Kaoru Mitoma again on the left and his chipped ball into the box was met by Evan Ferguson.

The young man hit a sweet volley which clipped the wrong side of the Everton post. It was another chance he should have done better with, but like Mitoma earlier we had reasons to forgive Ferguson not long after.

Ferguson almost had a goal before half time with an incredible shot from 25 yards out. It just brushed the top of Pickford's crossbar. Had it been on target, it surely would have gone in.

Sanchez had to make another intervention with a great save from Dwight McNeil to ensure Brighton went into the break ahead.

Little did we know what was about to unfold in the first 15 minutes of the second half. Ferguson scored what you would call a poacher's goal, popping a chipped cross from Sarmiento into the back of the net to give the Albion a 2-0 lead.

I enjoyed a celebratory cup of tea. Barely had a mouthful been swallowed and the cup put back on the table before Johnny was getting very excited about something March was doing, weaving in from the right.

March composed himself, got a low shot away, and beat Pickford diving to his right to make it 3-0. You must watch back the extended highlights and the expression on Roberto De Zerbi's face. It is quite a picture.

What happened next was also amazing. A strong Moises Caicedo challenge broke up an Everton attack, leaving the Toffees with the ball on the halfway line.

A really bad back pass enabled the Pascal Gross express train to poach the ball, race down the centre of the pitch, and beautifully chip over Jordan Pickford to score a goal despite the best efforts of Myolenko to clear the ball off the line.

Everton 0-4 Brighton and Pascal Gross running 40 yards with the ball to score. It was now embarrassing for the Toffees, something Warren was keen to tell us, as he said home fans were leaving in droves from Goodison Park.

Those who remained were so silent that Goodison began to resemble a library rather than a football stadium he said. Until the booing began again at the final whistle. Everton fans were not happy at all.

Three minutes were remaining when Everton fans had something finally to cheer about. Sanchez collided with Iwobi and as the Brighton goalkeeper got nothing of the ball only the man, referee Andre Marriner had no option but to award a penalty.

Such an error should be seen as a learning curve for Sanchez, who was denied a clean sheet when Gray converted to make it Everton 1-4 Brighton.

Then came those boos. Everton sunk into the relegation zone whilst Brighton climbed back into eighth place, full of confidence ahead of facing the red half of Liverpool at the Amex in our next Premier League outing.

From zero home goals for three months to nine in two away games

The FA Cup draw gave Brighton the longest trip of the third round, a five-hour and 20-minute drive to Middlesbrough according to Google Maps.

It was reported that those who made the journey earned a whole five loyalty points for their trouble! At least there were plenty of car parks around the Riverside Stadium; five I counted when looking on Google Maps.

As well as parking spaces, the stadium is located right next to the River Tees. The Tees leads into the North Sea, pointing the way towards Europe. Now that is a positive sign at the start of the Albion's FA Cup adventure, don't you think?

Brighton had last visited Middlesbrough five years ago, winning 2-1 in the fourth round of the same competition.

Johnny Cantor and Warren Aspinall seemed happy to be back

on Teesside and they once again provided amazing commentary for those of us back in Sussex.

They reported that Brighton had taken total control from the start. That led to an eighth-minute lead when the Albion's captain Pascal Gross scored.

Pervis Estupinan and Adam Lallana worked down the left and into the middle to find Evan Ferguson. He flicked onto an incoming Solly March running through the centre to bear down on Middlesbrough goalkeeper Zack Steffen.

Steffen made himself as big as he could and managed to deflect March's shot away — right into the path of Pascal Gross who made no mistake in slotting it home.

Adam Lallana had a shot himself which was saved by Steffen, after which it was the Albion's turn to make a mistake. Levi Colwill lost possession on halfway with Boro making the most of the opportunity.

Ryan Giles delivered a great cross from the right onto the head of Chuba Akpom. Jason Steele gets a hand to the ball but it managed to just about trickle over the line and into the goal.

Colwill shouldered the blame but like many of this Brighton team, he is young and learning. As was said in a post-match interview, the slightest of mistakes at this level of football and your opposition will score.

Watching back the highlights and Steele did not look best pleased with his efforts in keeping the header out, either.

Next came a long ball up the pitch from Steffen headed on by Matt Crooks. It fell to Riley McGree to hit a powerful shot which Steele was just able to tip over the bar. A great save from Steele which must have made up for any disappointment he felt about the goal.

Brighton went back on the attack and Kaoru Mitoma went down under very little contact from Tommy Smith on the edge of the Boro penalty area.

Referee Simon Hooper thought about it for a second or two and then awarded a soft free kick. Gross delivered and Steffen was not convincing with his punch going straight up into the air. Middlesbrough managed to survive.

Moises Caicedo had to intercept a Boro break to help Albion regain possession. Brighton began over the airwaves to sound more confident and in the 29th minute, regained the lead.

March played a good cross in from the right which Mitoma

met with a volley into the ground. The ball bounced over Steffen and Adam Lallana was on hand to head the ball into the net.

Had Lallana not made contact, then Evan Ferguson was also lurking in the right place at the right time as all good strikers do.

Half time arrived and Warren suggested that Brighton's play had been something on the slow side. Things seemed certain to quicken up when we were treated to the appearance of Alexis Mac Allister in place of Adam Lallana, something we discovered after the game had been planned to take place.

BBC Radio Sussex said that the Albion needed more intensity in the second half. And that is what we got right from the start, beginning with March having a header denied by Steffen.

Our World Cup hero did not take long to get involved. A drilled ball from Estupinan was diverted in with initial reports saying it had been a deflection off Mac Allister.

A closer look revealed that it was no deflection. Mac Allister had produced an intentional backheel flick to beat Steffen and make it 3-1. A great touch and a real class goal from a class player.

Roberto De Zerbi made further changes, swapping Danny Welbeck and Julio Enciso on for Ferguson and Mitoma. We later had the return of trusted defender Adam Webster, who replaced Colwill. Lewis Dunk enjoyed an afternoon off as he was rested ahead of a huge Premier League clash with Liverpool.

Mac Allister came close to his second of the game with a free kick just off target. Caicedo had earned the foul about 25 yards out but distance does not seem to matter to Mac Allister, who as we are getting to know is very dangerous from set pieces.

Having missed that free kick, Mac Allister did manage to complete a brace in the 80th minute when confidently putting away a Gross cross. That had me out of my seat and bashing those settee springs again.

A fifth and final Brighton goal arrived late on from Deniz Undav. It was great to see him on the pitch and scoring after being absent due to some personal issues in recent weeks. I am sure we all wish him well.

Even with a full-time score of Middlesbrough 1-5 Brighton, there was a lot of talk over how the Albion can improve after the game.

Johnny and Warren spoke about how the younger players

should perhaps not always go for glory themselves but look for a teammate who is better positioned. This was put down to the exuberance of youth with many of them still learning.

My biggest takeaway was that we had just seen Brighton score nine goals in two away games four days apart. It was not that long ago that we went three months without seeing an Albion goal at the Amex at all. The football since the return from the winter break has sure been enjoyable.

Having supported Brighton now for some 57 years, this is hands down one of the finest periods I can ever remember to be an Albion fan. Absolutely amazing.

Liverpool or Wolves next in the FA Cup and Brighton should fear neither team. The same goes for the next Premier League game against the Reds. Let us hope the good work and the goal-scoring continue.

Beating Liverpool 3-0 is the perfect medicine for a sprained ankle

Brighton v Liverpool was one of the most important games in the Albion's season so far and here I was, not even on the bench after suffering an injury in the build-up to the match.

It was not a tough tackle or a training ground knock that ruled me out, but rather an incident at the Ardingly Show Ground in Sussex.

I was walking our dog Teddy Boy, not even being distracted by looking at a phone or anything, when I missed a simple step on a damaged part of the Ardingly Showground tarmac roadway.

To the ground I fell, in excruciating pain. It was pouring with rain and there was nobody around to help, save an older lady.

She did very kindly come across and ask if I needed an ambulance. I replied, "Thanks for your concern, but they are all on strike today!"

I managed to get myself up eventually and hobbled the three-quarters of a mile back to my car with dear little Teddy Boy and then drove the short distance home. Good job it was automatic.

It was then that I realised I had an ankle the size of a junior match football. Next, I was driven to the wonderful minor injuries unit at the Queen Victoria Hospital in East Grinstead, where I was taken into their care.

I have nothing but praise for the team at the unit and I was away on crutches within an hour having been x-rayed and given the perfect advice for what had been diagnosed as a very serious sprain.

What a service! Rest was the only option and so I had to resign myself to the sofa, where I spent the rest of the week.

I had been hoping that come Saturday, the ankle would be healed enough, and I would be able to walk from the Bridge Car Park to the Amex Stadium.

Unfortunately, though, I failed a late fitness test and was nowhere near ready to hobble along for the game. I had been expecting it to be one of the most exciting matches of the season based on performances of late and so it proved.

The disappointment of missing the game was softened by our faithful BBC Radio Sussex commentary team of Johnny Cantor and Warren Aspinall.

Johnny and Warren always manage to create a good atmosphere. You could hear the Albion fans in fine voice behind them throughout the afternoon and no doubt that backing helped push the lads on.

Sky Sports did show a bit of the warmup from the Amex with the focus on new £45 million Liverpool signing Cody Gakpo, a 6'2 striker bought from PSV Eindhoven.

To my surprise, they showed Gakpo missing two shots in succession in the team warm-up. *That is a good sign* I thought and of course, Gakpo did not score at all during the game against the Albion.

Before kick-off, there was a tribute to Alexis Mac Allister. A big Argentina shirt was passed across the back of the North Stand as Mac Allister came onto the pitch to rapturous applause.

It sounded as though the appreciation was coming from Liverpool fans as well as Brighton. Mac Allister waved back to all four sides of the Amex with his World Cup medal proudly around his neck.

When the teams entered the field to the sound of Sussex by the Sea, I began to get quite excited. Brighton started strongly and the first highlight shown on the Albion website set the tone for the dominating performance that was to follow.

A great series of moves through Mac Allister, Adam Lallana, and Mac Allister again worked the ball to Solly March on the right side of the Liverpool area.

March let rip with his left foot, sending the ball to the far post where Trent Alexander-Arnold was very lucky that his touch sent the ball over the bar rather than into his own net.

A slick Pascal Gross corner found the head of Mac Allister who put the ball straight into the arms of Alisson Becker.

Next, it was the turn of Kaoru Mitoma to threaten. The Japanese Bullet Train put himself into top gear to accelerate away from Joel Matip. When Matip fouled Mitoma, referee Darren England had no choice but to get his yellow card out.

Liverpool made a rare attack when a long Alisson throw started a break which put Gakpo in. Robert Sanchez came out brilliantly to get to the ball, nearly sliding out of his area in the process.

Brighton then had another close shave when it needed more fine goalkeeping from Sanchez to prevent Mo Salah from opening the scoring.

The passing football of the Albion was frequently leaving Liverpool at sixes and sevens and unable to shut down space. Ian Wright pointed this out so well on *Match of the Day* where Brighton were even praised for their great football by Gary Lineker.

It was one of these passing moves that put March in to be brought down by Alisson. Mr England blew for a penalty, but VAR soon took charge and a check found an offside offence.

One final chance came in the first half when Moises Caicedo played a fantastic ball down the right for Solly March.

The highlights made it appear as if March had a third of the pitch all to himself which he charged into on a diagonal run, squaring the ball to Evan Ferguson whose shot was saved by Alisson.

I took a deep breath at half-time and wondered what might happen in the second half. Would the Albion find their breakthrough?

Yes, was the answer, and after only two minutes of kicking towards the North Stand. Matip played a poor pass intercepted by Alexis Mac Allister.

He moved the ball swiftly forward to Lallana before being knocked to the floor. Lallana flicked left to Mitoma, who saw March unmarked on the right.

In comes a great cross from Mitoma and March then beats Alisson to the ball to give Brighton a 47th-minute lead.

No time at all passed before the Albion added a second. I wondered if Johnny had hit the wrong button on his broadcasting device and was accidentally replaying the commentary of the first goal because it didn't seem feasible that March and Brighton could score again so soon.

This one was a belter from Solly March to round off another Albion move which cut through Liverpool like a hot knife through butter.

Sanchez made another brave save from Gakpo before Roberto De Zerbi started making substitutions. The squad are looking confident and strong right now shown by De Zerbi bringing on two players as good as Joel Veltman and Danny Welbeck.

Later changes saw Jeremy Sarmiento, Tariq Lamptey and Adam Webster come on. All were chomping at the bit to play their part and it was Welbeck who made it Brighton 3-0 Liverpool 15 minutes after coming on.

Veltman took a throw on the right to Solly March, and he flicked on to Danny Welbeck, who displayed two great touches to lift the ball over a defender and then volley it past Alisson.

Jurgen Klopp's face said it all. The final whistle sounded, and Brighton had another precious three points towards the dream of European football.

"What a time to be an Albion fan," said Johnny afterwards, and how right he is. Seeing Brighton flying high above Liverpool and Chelsea is enough to bring a tear to the eyes.

Who would have predicted back in August that this is how the table would look approaching the halfway stage of the season?

Next up is a trip to Leicester City, who lost 2-0 to Nottingham Forest at the weekend. The Foxes will be smarting from that, making them difficult opponents to face at the King Power Stadium.

There are no easy games in the Premier League but Brighton should fear nobody all the time they are playing football good enough to make the pain of a sprained ankle go away.

Halfway through the season and Europe is on the cards for Brighton

We have now passed the halfway mark in the 2022-23 season with European football still very much a possibility for Brighton through both the Premier League and the FA Cup.

Leicester City are a club that know a thing or two about

that, having regularly played in the Europa League and won at Wembley back in 2021.

Saturday's outing for those lucky enough to be able to attend was to visit the King Power Stadium. Brendan Rodgers' side had been on a bad run of late but they still posed enough of a threat to punish the Albion should Brighton make a mistake, as sometimes is the case.

Rodgers is no fool and a very astute tactician. We saw he had studied Roberto De Zerbi's style of play and did not want his players to commit to closing down, avoiding the Albion playing around them as they have so many teams since De Zerbi took over.

Foxes are cunning and they wait for the right time to pounce. Leicester certainly did that, making the 2-2 draw Brighton came away with a valuable point.

Still nursing my sprained ankle, I set myself up once again with BBC Radio Sussex broadcast. Johnny Cantor and Warren Aspinall were reporting live from a cold but bright and sunny Leicester, where Jan Paul Van Hecke was in the back four for his Premier League debut alongside Lewis Dunk, Pascal Gross, and Pervis Estupinan.

Having watched plenty of other Premier League sides since the winter break on television, Brighton must be one of the best for their current style of play.

Not only that, but they are playing so well so consistently. At some point, the Albion will surely have an off-day but for now, that does not seem to be happening.

Victory at the King Power would lift Brighton into fifth and a draw to sixth after Liverpool and Chelsea drew 0-0 in the lunchtime game.

Estupinan was marking his 25th birthday, so it was a happy birthday to Pervis! A football-related milestone is approaching for Lewis Dunk too, with Johnny reporting that this was his 395th appearance for the Seagulls. Five more and he joins a small club of players with over 400 games for the club. What a Captain he is, what a rock he has been. Long may he continue.

Over 3000 Brighton fans travelled to the King Power, and they could be heard loud and clear over the airwaves. Our commentators explained the Albion were keeping possession for the first few minutes and controlling the game as they settled into their normal rhythm.

Robert Sanchez and Lewis Dunk had to defend a cross that Dennis Praet could not quite get to Jamie Vardy, thank goodness. That move could have been a dangerous one.

My ears pricked up when I heard Mitoma had the ball down the flank and was weaving into the penalty area. Timothy Castagne did well to clear the ball off Mitoma for an Albion corner, which Pascal Gross found the head of Van Hecke with. He could not quite get the required angle on the header and over the bar, it went for a Leicester goal kick.

It was another Mitoma run in the 27th minute which opened the scoring and meant my settee springs took another bashing. Mitoma cut in from the left and bent the ball into the top right-hand corner for an absolute pearlier. The sort of finish you could watch back over a hundred times, and it would never get boring.

However, the 1-0 lead only lasted for some 11 minutes. Praet had gone off injured to be replaced by Marc Albrighton, who needed only two minutes to find the back of the Albion net.

Joel Veltman — himself a replacement for the injured Adam Lallana — and Dunk deflected away two Leicester attempts. The ball fell kindly to Albrighton, who stuck it underneath Sanchez to make it 1-1 going into half time.

Brighton should have had a penalty early in the second half when some impressive football including a fantastic back flick from Gross put Danny Welbeck into the area.

As Welbeck turned, his foot was kicked, and he was brought down. Referee Thomas Bramall did nothing and neither did VAR.

The replay showed it to be a clear penalty and the pundits on *Match of the Day* later in the evening agreed. Roberto De Zerbi remonstrated quite rightly, whilst Warren said he thought Mr Bramall must have left his yellow and red cards in the locker room.

Clearly, he hadn't, as De Zerbi was booked for protesting! There were other calls during the match which went overly in Leicester's favour, infuriating Warren to the point that he said: "The only way you would get handball from referee Bramall, is if you tried to take out the laces from the football!"

The Japanese Bullet Train Mitoma was off on another run again, racing into the area to set up a perfect chance for Solly March which only needed slotting home. Unlike last week against Liverpool, March skied that one right over the top of the bar.

That miss proved costly when Leicester broke, and Harvey Barnes took a shot that was deflected for a corner. The delivery came right towards the back post where Van Hecke swung a foot at it and missed.

Barnes was therefore left totally free to volley past Sanchez and Brighton were 2-1 down against the run of play.

The Albion now had 27 minutes to find an equaliser. Danny Ward saved from Solly March and Tariq Lamptey shot too high from a good Pascal Gross setup.

Next, it was Alexis Mac Allister's turn as some nice footwork took him past three Leicester players to pull the trigger. Ward though saved it with his legs.

Brighton were becoming more relentless, however. You cannot put into words the grit and determination this current Albion team have; as Winston Churchill once said, "Never ever give up" and they certainly do not ever give up!

A great cross came in from Pervis Estupinan it found the tall, towering figure of young Evan Ferguson, who headed into the far corner leaving Ward helpless to make it 2-2 in the 88th minute of the game. What a goal that was.

Not only did Brighton believe that they could equalise, but they also believed that they could now win it. Ferguson did not celebrate, instead, he grabbed the ball and ran straight to the centre spot. The Albion are not done yet, is what our teenager was saying, let's go again!

Had there been more than a few minutes remaining, I think Brighton would have gone on to win. Instead, it finished 2-2 and the Albion headed home in sixth spot in the table.

Warren was full of praise for Ferguson afterwards, even reporting that he was with the subs going through their routines after the final whistle. What enthusiasm the lad has to match the talent which we all hope will turn him into a great player.

As we say goodbye to Leandro Trossard, a door of opportunity opens for another player. The way that Brighton can seamlessly replace anyone who leaves means that Tony Bloom and Paul Barber deserve all our trust.

Roll on Liverpool in the FA Cup next week, where another route to Europe lies. I am starting to save for Wembley, so fingers crossed everyone!

Adam Lallana opened the scoring in Brighton's 3-1 Boxing Day
victory against his former club Southampton.

A brace from Solly March and a goal from Danny Wellbeck
gave Brighton a 3-0 win over Liverpool in January 2023.

Brighton's FA Cup run began with a 5-1 victory over Middlesbrough in January 2023.

Evan Ferguson scored the only goal of the game as Brighton
saw off Stoke City to reach the FA Cup quarter-final.

Danny Wellbeck scored 7 goals during the 2022-23 season.

Brighton thrashed Wolves 6-0 in May 2023 - one of the performances of the season.

Deniz Undav enjoyed a fine debut season for the Seagulls following his move from Union SG.

Roberto De Zerbi - what a man!

Roberto De Zerbi's backroom staff are a major factor behind Brighton's success.

A deflated Harry Haddock mascot after Brighton's 5-0 demolition
of Grimsby Town in the FA Cup quarter-final.

Warren Aspinall and Johnny Cantor provide top-notch coverage of all Brighton's games.

Brighton fans dressing up for the Seagulls first trip to the new Wembley stadium.

Author Tony Noble.

The Seagulls at Wembley in May 2023.

The boys warming up before the draw against Manchester City - the treble winners.

Captain fantastic. Lewis Dunk has represented Brighton in League One, the Championship and the Premier League. Next season he can add the Europa League to that list.

Two wins over Liverpool in 15 days — all things Brighton beautiful

Saturday 29th January 2023 was 39 years to the day at the old Goldstone Ground when Brighton famously beat Liverpool 2-0 to knock the all-conquering Reds out of the FA Cup.

The Albion goals that day came from Gerry Ryan and Terry Connor. The headline in the *Daily Mirror* sports pages on Monday read "All Things Brighton Beautiful" and the match report went on to say that Brighton were now Liverpool's bogeymen, having also knocked the Reds out of the FA Cup a season earlier at Anfield.

This time, the challenge for Brighton was to beat Liverpool twice in 15 days. And thanks to real grit, hard work, togetherness, and a willingness to never give up, they did.

As I am still nursing a severe sprain to the right ankle, I would have been unable to make the walk from the car park at the Amex to the East Stand and so it was the sofa for me once again.

Frustrating, to say the least. But such a high-profile game meant plenty of coverage with Johnny Cantor broadcasting on BBC Radio Sussex as normal and the match also live on ITV.

Clive Tydlesley and Ally McCoist were the commentators, but more thrilling was my hero Glenn Murray being a pundit. What fantastic insight he brought on the Brighton win.

ITV showed a great interview with Alexis Mac Allister before the game. What an impressive young man he is, who continues to show real loyalty to the Albion and gratitude for the way the club helped him to become a World Cup star.

Right from the kick-off it was all go. Naby Keita started an early Liverpool attack and Adam Webster made an important block in a melee followed by a goal-line clearance by Lewis Dunk.

Brighton also looked dangerous when they won the ball back. A great piece of play in midfield found its way to Solly March on the right.

He cut inside and put a low cross into the box which unfortunately fell to the wrong foot of Evan Ferguson, meaning a weak shot cleared off the line by Trent Alexander-Arnold.

A Solly March effort flew over the bar. Kaoru Mitoma flipped the ball to Ferguson, who touched back to Mitoma for a shot saved by Alisson but not cleanly.

Then the incredible occurred, Mo Salah breaking through the middle with the sort of chance we have seen him put away so many times in the past. This time though, he put the ball wide of Jason Steele's post.

Cody Gakpo put a ball into Mo Salah with Tariq Lamptey stepping up this time to make an interception. The ball slid back to Steele and right on cue, the Albion goalkeeper smothered it. Great stuff from Steele, as always.

It was fast turning into a classic cup tie when Liverpool scored their only goal of the game. Salah made the most of Dunk being out of position followed by a rebound off another player, slotting the ball through the gap left to Harvey Elliott.

The Liverpool youngster made no mistake and beat Jason Steele to give the Reds the lead with 30 minutes played.

Half time was fast approaching but the backing from the Amex was superb, and the crowd sounded in excellent voice, willing the Albion to find an equaliser before the break.

Ibrahima Konate gave away a corner that Brighton played short. When the ball was crossed into the box, it was headed away into space by Alexander-Arnold.

The space did not remain for long, however. Speedy Gonzalez Tariq Lamptey raced onto the ball and fired a shot into a group of players. It caught Dunk and deflected past Alisson, giving Rick O'Shea a goal for Brighton.

The Albion were attacking the North Stand in the second half and that seemed to inspire the players. Liverpool were the opposite and just seemed to become more and more desperate as the game went on. By the end, they resembled a group of bad players from a naughty boys' school.

A Dunk free kick crept just outside of the far post after Mac Allister was brought to ground in the first of a huge number of fouls the Reds committed.

Pascal Gross turned and shot a little too high over the bar following a great build-up by our Japanese Bullet Train Mitoma, weaving his way around the back before slotting through to Gross.

March ended up in the back of the net but could not take the ball with him. The cross he just failed to convert came once again from, yes you have guessed it, Mitoma.

Ferguson let one rip from close range but could not find the back of the net. At this point, I thought to myself it was only a matter of time before Brighton scored a second goal.

Liverpool must have been thinking the same as they became even more violent. Mac Allister was away on goal when Konate used his right elbow to clump our World Cup winner across the neck.

It happened just outside the penalty area and Konate had already been yellow-carded. How referee David Coote waved on is a mystery to this day.

An even worse foul came next from Fabinho. He came on in the 85th minute and by the 86th minute was booked for dragging his studs right down the back of Evan Ferguson's Achilles.

It was clear Evan Ferguson was in considerable pain and could not continue. Fabinho knew he should have been sent off, so much so that he laughed when the referee only showed a yellow.

Five minutes of added time were announced when Andrew Robertson produced another dirty Liverpool tackle to stop Mac Allister in his tracks.

Brighton never give up at the best of times and they certainly were not going to be kicked off the pitch if Liverpool felt that was the only way they could get a replay at Anfield.

Gross took the free kick and delivered the ball towards the far post. The running Pervis Estupinan let the ball bounce and chipped it back to the other side of the goal where Mitoma did a bit of juggling from left to right and volleyed home.

Watching on television, the noise which greeted the goal was so loud that it sounded like an explosion. Things quietened down when a VAR check was announced but after an agonising wait, it was deemed onside, and Brighton led 2-1 in the 92nd minute.

My settee springs were still taking a bashing and there was a tear in my eye when the game restarted. Liverpool would have to do more than hack down the Albion now and despite every red shirt desperately charging forward, Brighton held on to move into the fifth round of the FA Cup.

We know that we will face Stoke City, nicknamed the Potters. There is some irony that Brighton will have to overcome Potters to take a step closer to the FA Cup final. Maybe I will get to see the new Wembley before I snuff it! Fingers crossed.

CHAPTER 7
February 2023

Brighton's fighting spirit can carry the Albion into the top five.

HAVING NOT BEEN at the Amex since the Arsenal game on December 31st because of a January injury, I was in my seat for Brighton v Bournemouth a good 75 minutes before kick-off.

Boy, did it feel good to be back. Watching and listening from home and the football seems to have become even more exciting over the past month. It is truly a fantastic time to be an Albion fan. I wish my dad could have witnessed it.

Could things get even better before the end of the season? Beating Bournemouth — one of the most popular seaside resorts in the country, apparently — leaves Brighton sixth in the table having played 20 games.

Spurs in fifth are five points ahead but we have two games in hand. The tide could of course turn at any time and if it does, we must not get downhearted. But why not dream of finishing in the top five?

This Brighton squad have a genuine desire to win. Every game we see a determination to get a result with the past three matches against Leicester, Liverpool, and now Bournemouth all featuring late goals.

I watched a lot of football whilst stuck at home recuperating from my injury. It is obvious that the Albion put in a great deal more effort than many other teams, which will count for something by the end of the season.

And with 2022-23 looking likely to eclipse it, I am beginning to wonder if I need to start preparing for a second volume of Seagulls Best Ever Season should we be celebrating Europe or winning the FA Cup come June!

Before facing Bournemouth, I felt a little apprehensive, to be honest. The Cherries have won four of their last six visits to the Amex and as Roberto De Zerbi stated in his press conference on Friday, it would be a different game to Liverpool last week.

The sort of game the Albion have struggled with in the past. To win, Brighton would need to be on good form.

De Zerbi was undoubtedly right with his comments, a throwback if you like to when Graham Potter would always say there is never an easy game in the Premier League.

It appeared that Lewis Dunk lost the toss and so Albion were forced to play into the North Stand for the first half.

Joel Veltman started in the back four with Adam Webster taking a place on the bench whilst building back after injury.

World Cup winner Alexis Mac Allister was suspended by way of the yellow card top-up system and Moises Caicedo was amongst the substitutes following the January transfer window.

That gave Billy Gilmour the chance to join the midfield. Deniz Undav also stepped in up front with Evan Ferguson injured after the teenager was hacked down by Liverpool's Fabinho last week.

To win the game with players who have spent most of the season on the fringes so far shows how strong Roberto De Zerbi's squad is. Another reason to have faith that Brighton could overtake Spurs in the second half of the campaign.

It took Tariq Lamptey only one minute and 20 seconds to get down the right and cross. Bournemouth goalkeeper Neto looked to have problems as Danny Welbeck went for the header; however, referee Craig Pawson ruled in favour of Neto and denied Brighton a very, very early penalty.

The lively start continued when Chris Mepham flicked a corner into the Albion's side netting. It was very close to going in and a reminder of the threat that Bournemouth posed.

From the resulting goal kick came a marvellous piece of play by the Albion. Robert Sanchez went short to Lewis Dunk, who passed through the lines to Undav. Undav moved it beautifully to the right where Speedy Gonzalez Lamptey again raced away and crossed. Undav could not quite get to the return ahead of Neto, but what great football to go from one end to the other.

Then came one of the game's major talking points, those three shots in 10 seconds from Undav none of which unfortunately went in.

A very poor clearance from Neto saw him pass the ball straight to Undav, who moved immediately towards goal and swerved to the left to have a shot blocked on the six-yard line by a defender.

The rebound came straight back to Undav, whose second effort was saved by Neto. With his third attempt, Undav hit the left-hand post and Bournemouth survived the Undav onslaught.

Undav was so unlucky, but he did at least cause great excitement. If he keeps going, that first Premier League goal will not be far away.

Jefferson Lerma skied one over the bar at the other end, leaving Brighton fans to breathe a sigh of relief just like Bournemouth minutes earlier with the Undav chances.

Kaoru Mitoma nearly walked the ball in at the near post after some of his incredible dribbling. What a player he is, now a superstar in Japan and introducing Brighton to a worldwide audience.

A caller to BBC Radio Sussex a few days ago said they were on business in Japan recently, visiting several major cities.

After his work, he would go out in his Albion gear and be stopped frequently in the street by people who now knew of Brighton through Mitoma. Mitoma is regularly shown on Japanese television news for his exploits in the Premier League and there seem to be more wonderful fans visiting the Amex from Japan to support our club every week and spending money in the superstore.

It cannot be long until we have a Brighton shop opening in Tokyo, surely?! Whoever would have thought that the Albion would become so global?

Brighton's next chance came in the 38th minute when Welbeck headed a good cross from March straight at Neto. March then popped one too high and Welbeck was inches away from converting a ball in from Undav.

Half time arrived with the score at 0-0 and a feeling the game could still go either way. You could not fault the Albion's effort; it was just that the ball did not want to go in for them.

Brighton kept up the pressure after the break and Welbeck and Gilmour went close. For Gilmour, that was the end of his afternoon as Moises Caicedo came on.

Pervis Estupinan undoubtedly saved a Bournemouth goal with a brilliant sliding block which Sanchez was extremely grateful to him for.

Bournemouth squandered a couple more chances but as the game wore on, it appeared to be heading for a draw.

Except this is Brighton and in the 87th minute, Mitoma headed in a Jeremy Sarmiento cross to win it for the Albion after all those earlier opportunities had not gone our way.

Roberto De Zerbi was off on one of his jubilant runs down the line with his emotion there for all to see. He and the players did not feel like they had played at their best, but that is somewhat due to the high standards they have now set. Hopefully, that rolls into the Crystal Palace game on Saturday.

VAR's apology not good enough after Brighton were robbed.

What to do about VAR? In their 1-1 draw at Crystal Palace, Brighton were on the end of a decision caused by human error so bad that PGMOL director Howard Webb had to telephone the Albion and apologise for it.

A sorry from the refereeing board does not make up for the two points Brighton were denied. If we were to miss out on a new highest finish by two points at the end of the season, then it could be traced back to that moment at Selhurst. What use is an apology then?

Is it now necessary to speak out and say that more should be done when something like this happens? If a team is proven to have been on the receiving end of an incorrect decision because of human error using the technology which is there only to stop these things from happening, should that decision be reversed at a later date if it relates to a game-changing offside goal?

An independent panel of judges could rule whether the mistake was bad enough to warrant reversal and the goal reinstated. If the goal affects the final result, then tough. Why should players be denied points they have worked hard for?

It would be quite simple to add two more points to the Premier League table and adjust the final score accordingly after the game has concluded.

Bookmakers might complain, but they could just wait on disputed pay outs until PGMOL had given their final verdict. What do you think?

Still, Brighton were not the only team on the receiving end of an unfair decision from VAR on Saturday. Arsenal found themselves dropping points because the officials forgot to draw the lines to establish if Ivan Toney was offside when equalising for Brentford.

Not a good weekend for VAR. It was nice though to see Leandro Trossard doing well and scoring a valuable first-ever goal for the Gunners before the controversy.

Ironically with the problems VAR was to cause at Selhurst Park, I was pleased that Michael Oliver was the on-pitch referee. He has loads of experience and takes no nonsense, exactly what was needed in a game against Palace.

I was not able to be there so as normal, found myself tuning into BBC Radio Sussex. Johnny Cantor was joined by Warren Aspinall, who was back from a recent jolly away in the sunshine.

They told us that their view of the pitch was not the best, sitting right at the back and underneath the low roof of a stand that first opened in 1924.

Warren said before the game: "If we manage to keep a clean sheet, we will win." He had faith in Brighton scoring, and he would have been proven right had Robert Sanchez not made a mistake to give Palace their equaliser.

These things happen. David De Gea makes them, Hugo Lloris makes them. There is no point dwelling on it, just move on and support Sanchez like Roberto De Zerbi did after the game.

The Albion fans at Selhurst gave Sanchez a good reception at full-time. They were loud throughout the match and sounded brilliant over the airwaves, unlike the Palace support.

All you could hear was a beating drum which, as Johnny said, would drive you mad if you had to be near it for the full 90 minutes.

Listeners were also told that Palace had watered only one-half of the pitch before kick-off, presumably to give them some sort of advantage over Brighton. Is this gamesmanship fair?

There were three changes to the Albion team with Adam Webster, Alexis Mac Allister, and Moises Caicedo all back in the starting XI.

It did not take long for Alexis Mac Allister to have the first chance of the match. Solly March played a great ball through on the nine-minute mark but Mac Allister did not hit his shot with any real power and Vicente Guaita saved.

A second chance for Mac Allister then came when he tried

unsuccessfully to bend the ball around the Palace goalkeeper. Guaita saved again as the Albion showed that they really meant business.

Guaita next denied Kaoru Mitoma after a good ball from Lewis Dunk. Finally, in the 32nd minute brought a Brighton goal. . . or so we thought.

Pervis Estupinan scooped the ball over Guaita and into the right side of the Palace net for what would have been a very well-deserved first goal for the Albion.

Once Estupinan had finished celebrating, the VAR screen showed that it was being looked at. Stockley Park eventually told Michael Oliver to chalk it off for offside.

Except it wasn't offside. Estupinan had been in a perfectly onside position and the VAR operator had drawn the lines to the wrong Palace defender it was later discovered.

It took over two minutes for VAR to reach its decision and even then, they got it completely wrong. The only fair thing to do after such a terrible error is to reinstate the goal.

The decision seemed to deflate Brighton a little and Palace had their best chances after it. Webster made an amazing block following a Caicedo error to deny what looked a certain goal for Jean-Philippe Mateta.

Half time was reached with the score at 0-0. The stats however told the real story, Palace having had only one shot on target and 26 percent possession.

Brighton started the second half well and March had two chances in the opening four minutes. Evan Ferguson replaced Deniz Undav in the 57th minute and the Albion scored their second of the game soon after.

A great cross from Estupinan was volleyed in at the back post by March to leave Selhurst silenced with Brighton 1-0 ahead.

Unfortunately, the Palace fans were not silenced for long. A free kick into the Albion box looked safe as Sanchez leapt up to catch it.

The ball seemed to be in his hands when suddenly, he dropped it — and we all know what happens when a goalkeeper drops the ball. James Tomkins was left with the simple task of heading into the empty net.

Brighton now had 20 minutes to try and score a third goal to take all three points. Their best chances came in the final 10 minutes, starting when Pervis Estupinan who was chopped down by Abdoulaye Doucoure for Palace's fourth yellow card of the afternoon against the Albion's one.

Mac Allister missed the best Brighton opportunity, heading a Pascal Gross corner just wide of the post. At that point, you had to conclude this was one of those days where the ball was just not going to go in for the Albion. If it had, then the scoreline could have been 1-5 at least rather than Crystal Palace 1-1 Brighton.

The Albion will not have long to wait to show Palace how football should be played again with the sides to meet at the Amex on Thursday 16th March.

Hopefully, Palace will not be so lucky as to escape with a point thanks to Brighton being the victim of an unforgivable VAR error second time around.

Roberto De Zerbi right to speak about referee standards.

Two teams enjoying excellent seasons to date met at the Amex on Saturday. Fulham have surprised many people by challenging for Europe and we all know how well the Albion have been playing.

Brighton did not let us down as far as commitment and creating chances to score were concerned. It was just one of those games where the ball once again would not go into the onion bag, as our BBC Radio Sussex pundit Warren Aspinall is fond of saying.

Roberto De Zerbi will need a new vantage point for the FA Cup tie against Stoke City after being shown a red card in the tunnel following the final whistle.

De Zerbi then gave an interview in which he criticised the standard of refereeing in the Premier League only a few days after having a two-hour meeting with PGMOL chief Howard Webb.

Brighton were robbed at Crystal Palace by a VAR mistake, which is what brought Mr Webb to Sussex to see De Zerbi. One week later and referee Darren England gave an equally unfair performance.

De Zerbi was right to speak up against it and hopefully, PGMOL take on board what he said. I think some referees need to look at the legislation surrounding fairness which applies in the UK and throughout Europe and introduce it to their decision-making.

If Roberto does need a recommendation of where to sit for the Stoke match at the Bet365 Stadium, I can recommend getting as high up in the stands as possible.

My view from the East Upper is terrific. Being so elevated with the game playing out below may give De Zerbi a totally different outlook on his team.

Fulham boss Marco Silva recently went through the same experience that Roberto De Zerbi now faces when his passion on the touchline led to a red card and a one-match ban.

Marco Silva is clearly a good manager to have led the Cottagers to 10 wins already this season. Fulham defended better than most teams have managed against Brighton recently, digging in with their backs to the wall and taking their chance ruthlessly when Manor Solomon scored an 88th-minute winner.

Almost every Brighton player had a miss near the Fulham goal. Evan Ferguson was first with a shot that flew just over the bar.

Solly March was next. A great ball from Kaoru Mitoma set March off, he shifted onto his left foot and curled an effort that grazed the far post on its way out for a goal kick.

Joel Veltman had a shot deflected away for a corner. Alexis Mac Allister fired straight at Bernd Leno, guarding a goal he knows well from his disagreement with Neal Maupay when playing for Arsenal in 2020.

Fulham defender Issa Diop blocked from Ferguson. No matter what Brighton tried, they could find no way through and so the first half ended with the score at 0-0.

The Albion have been good at turning dominance into goals in the second half recently and you wondered what De Zerbi would say on this occasion to inspire a response.

Brighton were straight back into their groove immediately after the restart. Mitoma spun his magic down the right side and grabbed a corner by getting the deflection off Leno. From that corner came a Lewis Dunk header just wide. It was a golden opportunity that had slipped away, and Dunk knew it judging by his reaction.

It was edge-of-your-seat stuff. Veltman found himself in the Fulham box being clipped by Antonee Robinson. Mr England did not believe it to be a foul or penalty.

March finally popped the ball into the Fulham net but was immediately flagged offside. A high tackle from Andreas Pereira then left March on the ground but was shockingly ignored by Mr England. That decision from the referee nearly proved costly when Fulham countered and came close to scoring.

As the half wore on and Brighton were still struggling to find a goal, I began to wonder if this might be one of those games where the Albion were hit by a sucker punch on the break rather than grabbing a winner themselves.

Moises Caicedo missed an opportunity that flew just past the post. Mitoma went into the penalty area and was dragged to the ground, but this was not seen worthy of a penalty by Mr England either.

Substitute Tariq Lamptey worked wonders to link up with Facundo Buonanotte, whose attempt for the top left-hand corner was not a million miles away.

Buonanotte was a lot closer when he beat Leno to put the ball in the net from a Deniz Undav square pass, only for Undav to be flagged offside. For the second time, a Brighton goal was disallowed.

An Undav header flicked wide before Fulham found their winner. Undav and Buonanotte went for the same ball with possession returning to Fulham.

Carlos Vinícius put a fine pass through to Solomon whose charge towards goal could not be halted by Dunk, nor could Sanchez stop the shot.

The Cottagers led 1-0 and the game appeared to be over. Brighton though kept going and Mac Allister earned a free kick in a dangerous position.

It was a great strike from Mac Allister, the ball flying like a ballistic missile to beat Leno but crash into the stanchion.

Brighton now had a 10-day break to recover as the trip to Newcastle United has been postponed due to the Magpies' participation in the League Cup final. Hopefully, we might be due a better refereeing performance against the Potters in the FA Cup.

Imagine if Dunk gets an FA Cup to go with his 400 Brighton games.

The most important part of the Albion's FA Cup trip to Stoke City for me was Brighton game number 400 for our absolute rock and captain Lewis Dunk.

There have been some brilliant film clips on the Albion website and social media before and after the trip to the

Potteries, paying tribute to a man who has given everything for his hometown club and will continue to do so.

Dunk is a real credit to Brighton & Hove Albion as well as the city of Brighton. There is something extra special when a player born and bred in a town goes on to achieve everything Dunk has with his local team.

Having grown up in Hangleton myself, I feel like I can say for all We Are Brighton readers that we are so proud of Lewis and hope to see him play many, many more times for Brighton.

An FA Cup final might even be included in those future matches. A 1-0 victory against the Potters sent the Albion into the quarter-finals, where they will now face League Two Grimsby Town.

Imagine if Brighton beat Grimsby, win their semi, and go back to Wembley where Dunk lifts the trophy? What a fantastic way for an Albion great to mark 400 appearances for the club.

I could not make it to Stoke, however, nearly 3,000 of our dedicated away supporters did. Those who remained at home were treated to either the usual BBC Radio Sussex commentary with Johnny Cantor and Warren Aspinall or ITV4 televising live from the Bet365 Stadium.

Before the game, I had a weird feeling that Brighton would play well but end up let down by an error. Thankfully, that was not the case with the disappointment of the evening being to miss out seeing the Stoke City mascot Pottermous Hippo.

There was a minute of applause before kick-off for football commentator John Motson. A legend of the game whose voice accompanied so many great moments, he sadly passed away last week.

Lewis Dunk was quickly into the action in his milestone match, doing well to prevent Tyrese Campbell from putting the Potters 1-0 ahead early on.

Brighton began to work their way into the game after that. Tariq Lamptey crossed to the far post where Facundo Buonanotte came close to notching his first Albion goal with a header just wide.

Steele made another good save from Campbell trying his luck with a low shot from long range. Having kept two good Stoke chances out, Brighton went and took the lead with a quality goal.

The move started with, who else, but Dunk. His pass from

the back went straight through the Potters defence and into the path of the rushing Kaoru Mitoma.

The Japanese Bullet Train Kaoru Mitoma went around the Stoke right back and as home goalkeeper Jack Bonham came towards him, Mitoma played a pass across the box which gave Evan Ferguson a tap-in.

It was such a creative goal to watch featuring top-class football. If the Albion can keep conjuring up moves like that then my goodness, we have a great deal to look forward to over the next few months.

Steele continued to show his worth after Brighton went ahead, once again producing a cracking fingertip save to his right from Jordan Thompson.

Even with the Albion leading at the break, my feeling of dread remained. I was desperate for another Brighton goal to take the game away from Stoke.

The Albion's start to the second half did not help. Jan Paul van Hecke conceded a free kick which Axel Tuanzebe met with a header very close to creeping inside Steele's post for an equaliser.

That woke Brighton up and they were better from that point on. Mitoma could not quite squeeze home after Gross' delivery into the box was headed on.

The television pictures very clearly showed the Albion should have had a corner but referee Darren Bond incorrectly awarded a goal kick.

Danny Welbeck was given some minutes on his return from injury. His first attempt at goal was blocked, followed by Deniz Undav putting an effort towards an open goal wide with Bonham stranded miles off his line.

Another piece of great build-up gave Welbeck his second opportunity. Undav dummied for Welbeck to have a shot that hit the post.

Six inches to the left and Brighton would have wrapped the tie up. The woodwork thankfully did not prove costly as Stoke could find no equaliser and the Albion were through, one win from Wembley.

Can they now go all the way and do it for Dunk? Watch this space.

CHAPTER 8
March 2023

De Zerbi is the real final piece of the Brighton puzzle.

ROBERTO DE ZERBI appeared in a social media film clip recently saying, "The fans are the final piece of the puzzle". Really, it is De Zerbi who has been the man to take the Albion to another level.

The 4-0 win over West Ham United was a football extravaganza. I am still in shock from how well Brighton played; the quality of their football and the confidence running through the squad is so impressive.

When the team are in this sort of form, then the atmosphere normally follows. If Brighton are to make it to Europe, then it is our job to be the 12th man in every game between now and the end of the season.

Watching Liverpool beat Manchester United 7-0 on Sunday, I found it interesting that You'll Never Walk Alone is played immediately before kick-off with the players lined up on the pitch.

United had to wait to kick off until the anthem was finished. Imagine if we did that with Sussex by the Sea. It would have the Amex singing at the first whistle and might encourage the West and East Stands to help the North turn up the volume by continuing into the game itself.

Brighton made a fast start against West Ham without needing too much vocal encouragement. Solly March weaved through four, yes four, West Ham defenders to shoot just wide.

The lack of Roberto De Zerbi storming around his dugout at this match was noticeable. De Zerbi was serving a one-game touchline ban and he looked very snug in a warm coat and scarf up in the director's box, with his mobile in hand.

He remained in contact with the bench via his mobile phone, where assistant manager Andrea Maldera was doing the job of organising the troops.

March was again involved as Brighton took the lead with a quarter of an hour played. He hit a long cross ball to Kaoru Mitoma on the left.

Mitoma beat Ben Johnson to move into the penalty area where he was pushed by Jarrod Bowen and tumbled to the ground.

Referee Stuart Attwell had a good view and gave a penalty for the clumsy interaction by Bowen. Hammers goalkeeper Alphonse Areola went the right way, but Alexis Mac Allister hit the spot kick with too much power right into the top left corner. 1-0 to the Albion.

De Zerbi had given Jason Steele just the second Premier League start of his career. Steele was soon making a fantastic save from Bowen to prevent West Ham from equalising.

Adam Webster is some way ahead of Steele and this was his 100th Premier League appearance. He made a good intervention on Danny Ings to remind everyone why he is one of the most dependable players that Brighton have.

Half time arrived with the score at 1-0. Both sides could have scored more, and I was a little worried that the lead was only one goal and maybe short-lived.

The smash-and-grab that Fulham pulled off last time at the Amex was still in my memory; what if West Ham repeated the trick with an underserved equaliser or worse?

There was no need to worry, however. I understand De Zerbi visited the Albion dressing room at half time and whatever he said worked wonders as the Albion were magnificent in the second half.

While Roberto De Zerbi was giving his half time team talk, we were all treated to Leonardo Ulloa being on the pitch. It was great to see him looking so well. I wonder if he spent the game wondering how many goals, he could score in this Brighton team.

Ulloa would have easily put away the second Albion goal, netted seven minutes after the break by Joel Veltman. Alexis Mac Allister did one of his cheeky back heel flicks which had to be deflected wide for a corner.

Pascal Gross took the ball and Joel Veltman chested into

the empty goal at the back post. Not one West Ham player had picked him up. It was shocking defending, and you could understand the frustration of the visiting fans.

Brighton were starting to motor now. Young Evan Ferguson let off a sweet shot from the right that needed a great save from Areola. Nayef Aguerd then produced a last-man tackle to deny Ferguson a tap in.

Albion goal number three was the result of some glorious football. Gross crossed from the right and Mitoma the Japanese Bullet Train arrived at the far platform with perfect timing to slide the ball the correct side of the post.

Julio Enciso was deprived of his first Brighton goal by a flying save onto the bar from Areola. It fell to Danny Welbeck to add the fourth, firing a low shot through a group of players and into the far corner of the net.

The football was brilliant and the whole afternoon was wonderful entertainment. Brighton are starting to play like a top-four side and it is largely down to that man Roberto De Zerbi.

It is enough to bring a tear to the eye. These players have the belief, the skill, the determination, and the coaching team to continue to improve.

The infrastructure around them is generating success and that comes right from the top. Brighton must be the envy of most of the Premier League right now as we head to great heights under the management of the master Roberto De Zerbi.

Other results show it was a good point at Leeds.

Brighton visited Elland Road for a match against the Peacocks in a great place as recent performances have been absolutely incredible.

The football has been exciting and there have largely been plenty of goals too, like last week when the Albion put four goals past West Ham.

Leeds was always going to be a difficult place to visit. Some real greats of the game have played for them down the years and the crowd at Elland Road when it gets behind their team is their 12th man.

We all know that in any kind of sporting arena, you get days or games when things do not go as well as you hope. That was the case against Leeds as although Brighton played some good football, a couple of errors cost them all three points.

However, any point away from home is a good one. You only have to look at the results of the Albion's rivals for European places to see this.

Arsenal gave Brighton a helping hand by beating Fulham 3-0. Bournemouth were 1-0 winners against Liverpool. Brentford went down 1-0 away at Everton.

All in all, drawing 2-2 at Leeds took us up a slot in the league to seventh place and we now stand at 39 points. If Brighton beat Crystal Palace at the Amex in midweek, the table will be looking very good by the time the FA Cup quarter-final tie against Grimsby Town at the Amex takes place on Sunday.

I was an "Albion Online Virtual Away Supporter" for the match at Elland Road with budget cuts meaning it was a Saturday spent in North Sussex rather than North Yorkshire.

BBC Radio Sussex as always did a great job in bringing the action to those of us not in Leeds with Johnny Cantor, Warren Aspinall, and Adrian Harmes keeping everyone up to date.

Our commentators reported early on that the Albion were a little sloppy with their passes and not being quite as clinical as they had been of late.

A few chances were not converted by Brighton whilst Luke Ayling made his presence felt for the Peacocks twice in a matter of minutes. His second attempt was beautifully intercepted by Kaoru Mitoma and then saved well by Jason Steele.

Brighton took the lead on 33 minutes thanks to some great work by Pascal Gross down the right side. He turned and crossed and Mitoma headed back across the goal to leave Alexis Mac Allister a simple header which he dealt with beautifully to beat Illan Meslier.

It was a goal created by brilliant football and which gave us another classic line from Warren: "Gross rolled his opponent like a tin of John West Salmon".

The Albion were not ahead for long. A ball on the right was lost by Joel Veltman. It looked as if it was going to roll out of play, only for Jack Harrison to keep it in.

Harrison squared to Patrick Bamford, who let a shot go from a few yards outside the penalty area. It flew like a bullet over Steele, hitting the underside of the bar and bouncing into the goal.

The Peacocks now had their tails up and raced forward again through Bamford. This time, his shot went into the side netting.

Alexis Mac Allister then missed a sitter just before half time when shooting wide from 12 yards out after a good run and cross down the left from Mitoma.

Johnny told us after the referee's whistle had blown that Brighton have not been at their best in the opening 45 minutes, which sounded like a fair comment.

The second half did not begin in much better fashion. Steele was called upon to make a great save, getting his right hand to a low effort and just managing to push it past his post. Leeds were putting on the pressure and Elland Road was becoming noisier.

It was against the run of play slightly when the Albion took the lead with 61 minutes played. Yet another dangerous run and a cross from Mitoma bumped around the Leeds defence and Meslier before finding its way into the back of the net.

Initially, it looked as though March had helped put it over the line. Eventually, the final touch was credited to Harrison and so it went down as an own goal.

That spurred Brighton on. A surging run from Pervis Estupinan and cross could not quite be turned in by Evan Ferguson. March had a left-footed half-volley saved by Meslier diving to keep it out of the bottom corner.

Danny Welbeck came on and almost scored twice. A piece of brilliance saw him beat a defender but the finished product was not quite there as it flew too high and wide.

Welbeck then nearly steered the ball past Meslier with the Leeds goalkeeper doing well to get a touch and divert the ball away.

I was surprised that Wilfried Gnonto only started on the bench for the Peacocks. In the Leeds games I have watched on television, he has been one of their most creative players. I was therefore a little wary when he replaced Crysencio Summerville after 66 minutes.

Gnonto was involved in the Leeds equaliser 12 minutes later. He took a quick corner to Jack Harrison, whose turn and shot from the left dipped high and fast over Steele and into the net.

Brighton appealed that there were two balls on the pitch when the corner was taken. However, the goal was allowed to stand. Some say the Albion were caught napping; I say, after seeing the goal that it was really a bold shot which paid off for Leeds.

The Peacocks might have won it late on. Adam Webster was already in great pain after an earlier challenge and still managed to save the day, preventing Leeds from breaking and scoring a third.

And so, the final whistle blew with it finishing Leeds 2-2 Brighton. The Peacocks strutted off the happier of the teams with Albion not having the best of days and yet still gaining a point and moving up a place in the table. Now for Wednesday evening.

The Seagulls logo brings Brighton fans together wherever they are.

A few hours before Brighton took on Crystal Palace at the Amex and there was a gathering of Albion supporters at Ardingly Sussex County Showground.

It happened purely by chance. We were all enjoying the Wednesday morning air when the Seagulls logo on our clothing brought us all together.

Paul Barber had been on BBC Radio Sussex earlier in the day talking to Alison Ferns. Here I found myself shortly after chatting with Mr Barber's PA's husband, and also a lifelong Albion fan Mr Dave Hill.

Dave agreed to a selfie and said he has supported the Albion since the 1960s. He no longer attends in person but listens via BBC Sussex.

This shows just how important the service local radio provides to fans who cannot get to the Amex; many of us rely on Johnny Cantor & Warren Aspinall and any moves to take them off the broadcast schedule have to be avoided.

Unarranged meetings like these between Brighton fans are happening all over the world now; from Ardingly Showground to Tokyo, where Kaoru Mitoma has turned the Albion into a household name. The Brighton badge has never been so powerful.

Later that evening and it was off to the Amex for a journey wonderfully dealt with by Seagull Travel. I boarded the coach at Burgess Hill railway station and it took the driver no time at all to make all the pickups followed by excellent progress to the stadium.

On arrival, there were already a lot of Palace fans caged in the South Stand. They were in great voice, even as news started to spread that their third-choice goalkeeper would be playing.

Injuries to Vicente Guaita and Sam Johnstone meant 19-year-old Joe Whitworth would be making his Palace debut. It turned out to be a good evening for him (if not Palace) as only Solly March managed to find a way through.

It was a damp night, and you could see the rain passing in front of the floodlights. We were treated to a light show and fire display just before kick-off as Brighton prepared to set about ending a run of over four years and seven games since beating their long-time rivals.

Palace came flying out of the starting blocks, catching Brighton players and fans by surprise. The first 15 minutes saw the Albion well and truly on the back foot.

Wilfried Zaha had an early run down the right, a couple of stepovers thrown in and causing Jason Steele to push a shot away for a corner.

Kaoru Mitoma made a good block at the expense of another Palace corner. The Eagles played it short onto the head of Odsonne Edouard who narrowly missed Steele's far post.

Steele next denied Michael Olise. Nobody would have predicted at that point with the way Palace were playing that 48 hours later, the Eagles would be sacking Patrick Vieira their head coach.

Brighton had their first real effort when a run down the left by Pervis Estupinan saw the ball slipped left to Kaoru Mitoma. He let a shot go but unfortunately, it was straight at Whitworth.

Mitoma was beginning to make the Amex bounce. Another Japanese Bullet Train ran down the left fed Solly March to hit an effort from the right side of the box.

Whitworth had no chance, and the ball flew into the back of the net. In the 15th minute on the 15th day of March, Solly had given Brighton the lead over Crystal Palace.

I have never been so relieved as I was to see that goal go in. It was a great finish and it felt like an important one as it came against the run of play.

The Albion were beginning to get on top now. Cheick Doucoure denied Danny Welbeck when clearing as Welbeck went to tap home a low Pascal Gross cross into the box.

Steele had to make a great save from Edouard racing through the middle. Lewis Dunk looked at the assistant referee to ask why there was no offside flag; it felt dangerous asking the officials for help when leading only by one goal and Palace looking a threat.

Doucoure was lucky to stay on the pitch when already on a yellow card and fouling Moises Caicedo. However, referee Peter Bankes refused to book Docoure and so he survived until half time when he was substituted by Vieria.

The second half began with Brighton playing towards the North Stand. Whitworth saved an early Estupinan shot with his left leg before we were treated to an unplanned light show.

For a few seconds, the whole Amex was plunged into darkness. Apparently, there had been a power surge that impacted the whole area.

Brighton fans responded by turning on their phone torches, seeing the West Stand all lit up was quite the picture.

Alexis Mac Allister had a shot well saved by the young Palace goalkeeper followed by a big mistake at the other end almost letting the Eagles equalise.

Steele was caught passing out from the back but fortunately, the Palace effort on goal missed the target. A lucky escape ahead of nine minutes of injury time.

When the full-time whistle eventually blew, the Amex roared. It was a noise of relief more than anything else, made up of Brighton finally beating Palace and doing so when not playing near their best.

The boot is normally on the other foot with the Albion drawing or losing against Palace when they do not deserve to — leaving plenty more to talk about when strangers meet in public drawn together by the Seagull badge over the coming week.

Brighton did well in making Grimsby's big day extra special.

A fantastic week for the Albion was rounded off on Sunday with the visit of League Two side Grimsby Town to the Amex for the FA Cup quarter-finals.

It was a big day out for Grimsby fans, or maybe even a weekend? The visitors were reported to have arrived in Brighton on Saturday, enjoying a south coast seaside rather than an east coast seaside.

They came in their thousands, over four thousand in fact. There was a fantastic atmosphere and that made the Amex an exciting place to be, especially if you were a mum being treated to a Mother's Day at the football.

The noise that the visitors created was unlike anything I have ever heard from any group of away supporters. It was relentless until the goals started going in, but even then, they kept cheering their team on. You could tell how proud the Grimsby players had made their town with their FA Cup heroics.

If they start playing like that in the league with the same sort of support behind them, there will be something fishy going on if they don't begin moving up the table.

Brighton tried to make the day extra special for the Grimsby supporters. I am led to believe that the Mariners' mascot was the great-grandson of a Grimsby player from the 1930s.

Some memory he will have when he grows up and tells his great-grandchildren of when Grimsby played in the FA Cup quarter-finals.

It will be the same for the Mariners players, who swapped shirts with the Albion and were given a standing ovation as they walked off from a lot of Brighton supporters who remained in the ground.

The Albion paid out for both North and South Stands to have coloured cards which formed patterns welcoming both teams to the pitch. What a lovely gesture that was.

Mariners' fans afterwards had nothing but praise for the Amex, the Albion, and the helpfulness and kindness showed to them by Seagulls fans.

The only let down was that a number of Grimsby supporters were very untidy. The pitch ended up being a rubbish tip for anything they could get their hands on; those cards, their inflatable haddocks, I even heard coinage was thrown onto the pitch.

Thankfully, referee Jarred Gillett stopped the game to get something done about it in the second half. Brighton were already on their way to Wembley at this point, and so I did wonder if they might just give Robert Sanchez a bin liner and have him pick the rubbish up for something to do.

Speaking of Wembley, I have never seen the Albion play there. I was especially desperate for Brighton to win and as such, re-watched the game as soon as I got home. Having my hero Glenn Murray as part of the BBC punditry team made it almost as enjoyable the second time around!

I was a little concerned at times during the first half when the game was a slow burner with a long fuse. Roberto De Zerbi was watching from the West Upper but once he was able to say a few words to the players at half time, Brighton caught light.

As play re-commenced, it became clear Grimsby were going to go long at every opportunity from goalkeeper Max Crocombe.

That meant Lewis Dunk, Adam Webster, Pervis Estupinan, and Moises Caicedo were busy making more headers in one half of football than they probably have all season so far combined.

It did not take Brighton long to take the lead. Some possession football ended with a low grass-cutting shot from Caicedo.

Crocombe saved, only for the rebound to fall nicely for Deniz Undav to score a poacher's goal. Six minutes gone and the Albion led 1-0.

Brighton continued with their patient passing football. It released Kaoru Mitoma down the right to speed off like a Japanese Bullet Train.

Mitoma's cross looked perfect until it was intercepted by a Grimsby defender, just preventing Solly March from doubling the lead.

Those Mariners fans who waved their inflatable Harry Haddocks in the air nearly had something to cheer when Sanchez went to scoop up a ball on the very edge of his area. VAR checked and Sanchez was eventually ruled to have handled inside the box rather than outside. Sanchez was lucky as it looked like he had made a serious mistake.

The Grimsby goal began to resemble a fairground shooting arcade after that. Mitoma, Caicedo, and Pascal Gross all missed before half time.

Caicedo was caught from behind by a defender as he shot and seemed to be suffering from back pain. I was pretty impressed he soldiered on, especially with a long flight to Australia for international duty with Ecuador ahead of him. Going short-haul with a bad back is a struggle enough, let alone to the other side of the world.

During the break, we were treated to hearing about all the amazing work the medical team at the Amex have achieved over the past 10 years.

In that time, seven people we were told had suffered a cardiac arrest. I was amazed and relieved to hear that all seven had been saved, an incredible 100 percent success rate for the Albion medical team.

The doctor and his team of response staff with their defibrillators deserve all the praise they can get. At my age, you hope you are not going to be their next patient.

You could tell straight from the start of the second half that De Zerbi must have had words at half time. There was much more energy and determination to get the job done and see us on our way to Wembley Stadium.

March played a high-dipping ball towards the Grimsby goal which bounced off the post and to Denis Undav. He somehow lashed it over the bar from six yards out when it really should have gone in.

A piece of Evan Ferguson magic gave Brighton their second goal. Alexis Mac Allister played a lovely pass into Ferguson, who brought it down, turned, and gently found the right-hand corner with such a controlled finish.

Mitoma worked his way into a dangerous space again to let a shot go which missed the far post by a ball's width. Then Ferguson had a goal disallowed when Solly March had a toenail offside as he played the final pass.

Sanchez had to take a break from dodging litter to make a strong save from John McAtee with Webster cleaning up the rebound.

Grimsby were becoming more of an attacking force and that meant the game began to resemble a classic end-to-end cup tie heading into the closing stages.

Mitoma raced into the box and appeared to be clipped by Michee Efete. No penalty was given but having watched back the highlights, I felt Mitoma deserved to win a spot kick.

Brighton instead settled for a corner which Gross delivered and Webster headed against the woodwork. The whistle blew for some sort of foul in there, giving Grimsby a chance to catch their breath and take a break for a minute.

The Albion were now applying relentless pressure and it soon took its toll. Ferguson finished with pinpoint accuracy to make it 3-0 in what was his last action of the game with Danny Welbeck coming in.

Ferguson clearly wanted his hat trick, judging by the fact he kicked the ball away from the centre spot as he was being brought off.

Such enthusiasm from a young player is great to see, even if

Brighton were doing the right thing by protecting him ahead of what is sure to be a busy set of internationals with the Republic of Ireland.

Welbeck was soon into the game, having a shot smothered by Crocombe after picking up a pass from the right by March. Crocombe then parried away another Welbeck effort.

March then disappeared from his normal right flank, suddenly popping up on the left where he launched himself at a cross from Webster to score his eighth goal of the season with a superb diving header to make it 4-0.

Sanchez was called into action again by McAtee and young midfielder Yasin Ayari came on for his debut. I was really impressed by Ayari, who already looks like he has the potential to play exciting and creative football.

Mitoma rounded off the scoring with a heavily deflected fifth. Brighton 5 Grimsby Town 0. Wembley beckons now and I have already booked my Seagull Travel tickets. . . now I just need a match ticket! Bring on Manchester United.

CHAPTER 9
April 2023

You cannot take your eyes off Brighton under De Zerbi for a minute.

IT WAS A dash back from Devon for the Nobles on Thursday afternoon for two reasons. The first was to avoid the horrible weather which was coming in for the weekend in the South of England.

The second was to be ready and waiting in place at 9 a.m. Friday morning, sat at the computer to buy our FA Cup semi-final tickets.

Fortunately, all went to plan, and we are off to Wembley on Sunday 23rd April. Having seen Manchester United well beaten by Newcastle United at St James' Park, Brighton have nothing to fear when we face Erik ten Hag and co, for a place in the Emirates FA Cup final.

Brentford at the weekend was always going to be a tough game. Not only are the Bees having their best-ever season, but there is a lot of rivalry at board level between Tony Bloom and Matthew Benham as underlined in the build-up on We Are Brighton.Com website.

I, for one, was not 100 percent confident. Ivan Toney and Bryan Mbeumo were sure to give the Albion defence a hard time, making it likely we would see goals. Never did I imagine there would be six of them — and in such an exciting manner.

The sun was out, and Spring was in the air. Soon, we will be coming to the Amex in short sleeve shirts again. I would never go so far as to appear bare-chested at this time of year, like those members of the Toon Army cheering their side to victory against Manchester United.

Two weeks off now for the international break had left the pitch looking great, although the ground staff may have found themselves picking up pieces of a broken iPad from it after Roberto De Zerbi gave Andrea Maldera's tablet a right clobbering in frustration at Brentford scoring their third goal.

Still, at least he was not venting his frustration at the referee, who on this occasion was Michael Oliver. I was happy to see one of the best officials in the country taking charge, hoping he would not stand for the time-wasting and other gamesmanship which visiting teams have used against Brighton this season.

So much happened in this game that you could not take your eyes off it for a minute. De Zerbi and the squad are serving up such entertainment for us, which is making the Albion's attempts to qualify for Europe even more exciting.

The action started straight from kick-off. Pervis Estupinan played in Kaoru Mitoma, who was halted by a great tackle from Brentford defender Ethan Pinnock.

Not long after that and the Bees took the lead. Mathias Jenson threw to Mbeumo, collected the return, and crossed into the box.

There was Pontus Jansson, making his first start since October and climbing highest in the air to head a rocket over Jason Steele.

The Albion players looked stunned, and the crowd was silenced. Not like our friends from Grimsby Town in the previous game at the Amex, who kept chanting even as their side fell four and five goals behind.

We must all remember when we go to Wembley, yes all of us, to be in good voice and support the lads no matter what.

Brentford are unbeaten in all 31 Premier League matches that they have taken the lead in. I began to feel a bit uncomfortable at this point and wondered whether Brighton could be the team to end that impressive statistic. We nearly did, by the end of the game.

Next came from the right side of an indirect free kick in the penalty area resulting from Estupinan cutting out Mbeumo and Steele picking up the loose ball.

The free kick was not only well blocked by Brighton but nearly set up an attack. Estupinan broke up the right with Brentford doing well to eventually stop the counter.

Bees' goalkeeper David Raya made the first of many saves when keeping out a left-foot Solly March shot. Lovely football from Steele to Joel Veltman to Pascal Gross to March that created the chance.

Raya proved to be the best Brentford player on the pitch that day, saving his team numerous times over the course of a match in which Brighton were the better team. . . although you would expect me to say that!

The first Albion equaliser came when Steele played a perfectly judged pass over the top of the Bees defence. Mitoma ran through and lobbed the ball over Raya to make it 1-1 with a goal made from fantastic foresight from Jason Steele to play the pass and fantastic foresight from Mitoma for the controlled finish.

De Zerbi did his little dance which was great to see. The happiness did not last long; however, I was still celebrating the Albion goal when Brentford scored at the other end.

A throw from Joel Veltman was intercepted. Two Brentford touches later and Toney found himself in beating Steele one-on-one. The bloke running the Albion scoreboard was struggling to keep up.

Brighton showed that they were not happy about the situation by equalising again, just six minutes later this time. Danny Welbeck headed down and into the Brentford goal with a cross from, yes you guessed it, Solly March who cannot seem to stop scoring or assisting.

Four goals in 29 minutes. A bit of a lull followed, allowing us to all catch our breath. Brighton had further chances before half time from Mitoma, Alexis Mac Allister, and Levi Colwill but there were no further additions to the score.

During the interval, I stuffed my traditional bag of wine gums into my mouth in record time as I needed sustenance to keep going. It was edge-of-the-seat stuff in the East Upper Stand, so goodness knows how the players in the middle of it all felt!

The decision to eat all those wine gums proved a good one as the action kept going. Mbeumo lined up a free kick in the 48th minute and I began twitching. Every time this dangerous Bee was near the ball, something seemed to happen.

In came the perfect delivery towards the far post where Pinnock sneaked in unnoticed and volleyed home left-footed. Brighton 2-3 Brentford and there were still 41 minutes plus added time to play.

It was all Brighton after that with too many chances to mention. Moises Caicedo, March, Veltman, Gross, and Lewis Dunk were all kept out by David Raya, who continued to try and save the day for Brentford.

The last minute brought a chance for Deniz Undav who went over the bar from close range. There was an unexpected appeal for handball, VAR looked, and Mr Oliver was soon sent to the monitor.

He checked the situation and awarded Brighton a penalty. The decision seemed to take ages to reach and left Mac Allister standing and waiting for some time at the penalty spot awaiting the referee's decision.

Mac Allister remained completely unflustered, stepped up, and rocketed the ball into the top corner to make it Brighton 3-3 Brentford. What a penalty it was and a brilliant way to level the game.

The Albion deserved at least a point and it would have been more, had they not conceded goals from so many errors. Mistakes need not be a bad thing as you learn from them, and the most important thing was that Brighton did not lose the game.

Mr Tony Bloom was a happy man, seen dancing in the aisles when the Alexis Mac Allister penalty hit the net. After celebrating the goal, I was absolutely worn out.

The trudge back to the Bridge car park seemed much harder than normal, it nearly finished me off! That is the price we pay though for an exciting manager and an exciting team, who you cannot take your eyes off without risking missing something!

So much water under the bridge since losing 5-0 to Bournemouth.

Before Tuesday night, Brighton had not beaten Bournemouth for some considerable time at their stadium. 16 years to be precise and only twice in 30.

This was a game of football that could have gone awfully wrong. The Albion however came through and did so well to keep at bay a Cherries side desperate for points as they fight off the threat of relegation.

I was not very confident, myself. I still remember the bashing they gave us at the Amex under Chris Hughton when winning

5-0. One of the worst days of the past 10 years to be a Brighton fan.

So much water has passed under the bridge since then, however, can it really be only four years ago that happened? Who would have thought leaving the Amex that day we would be talking about Brighton challenging for Europe above Chelsea and Liverpool in the table?

We now have a squad with nothing to fear from any team. Before, a trip to Spurs would have been met with some trepidation. Now Brighton go to the Tottenham Hotspur Stadium confident of getting a result and winning.

Spurs looked dreadful against Everton on Monday night and somehow became even worse when the Toffees went down to 10 men. Tottenham then followed suit in having Lucas Moura sent off, so he misses the Albion's visit to North London.

A very late, superb goal from Michael Keane mirrored that famous Vincent Kompany strike for Manchester City a while back to give Everton a deserved draw which moves Spurs closer into our sights.

Like many of you, I could not make the midweek trip to the Vitality Stadium. It was down to BBC Radio Sussex to relay what was happening, via Johnny Cantor and ex-Albion striker Warren Aspinall.

Johnny, Warren, Adrian Harmes and all the team do sterling work in keeping us informed as to how the Seagulls are doing, and long may that continue.

With the radio on, I also turned the television onto Chelsea against Liverpool and watched on mute. How would Bruno perform in his first game as caretaker manager for Chelsea? The answer was that both sides were awful. Brighton need not worry about either in the race for Europe.

The strength of the Albion squad was shown through Roberto De Zerbi resting Levi Colwill and Danny Welbeck. Adam Webster came in at the back and Evan Ferguson up front.

Before kick-off, Johnny and Warren had to do their best fighting to be heard over nightclub disco music being blasted around the Vitality Stadium.

Warren told us of the days when he played for Bournemouth when club representatives walked around the old Dean Court with buckets trying to raise money for wages and other club necessities.

This took me on a flashback to the Goldstone Ground as a child. I am sure I remember a similar thing happening when I was 11 years old in 1966, or maybe I am dreaming. Even so, both Brighton and the Cherries have come a long way since then.

I was twitchy before kick-off, knowing that the first goal would be crucial. If Brighton could score and then add a second as quickly as possible, that would settle all the nerves stemming from the Albion's poor record against Bournemouth.

There were a couple of early halts in play, one for religious reasons and the other because referee Darren Bond had problems with his communication kit. This has happened several times at the Amex this season.

Brighton had to withstand a couple of early attacks before we heard the cry of "GOAL" in the 28th minute. And what a goal it was too.

Lewis Dunk passed down the left to Pervis Estupinan who crossed. That was blocked with the rebound falling to Kaoru Mitoma.

He squared to Ferguson, who impudently backheeled the ball into the bottom left corner without even looking at Bournemouth goalkeeper Neto.

At 18 years old Evan Ferguson, is a fantastic talent. He had so much skill and confidence and is certainly going to become one of the best strikers to have played for Brighton and Hove Albion.

The Albion had a bit of a bad patch after taking the lead, giving the ball away too often and causing problems for themselves.

Jason Steele made a great save from Dominic Solanke and then another from the same player with a second attempt which was cut out beautifully by Adam Webster.

Hamed Traore put wide missing a massive opportunity for the hosts. Thank goodness, I thought to myself, although the worried tone creeping into the voice of our commentators suggested Brighton might need a few more let-offs from Bournemouth.

The Albion did, however, make it to half time 1-0 ahead. They might have moved 2-0 ahead when Ferguson pivoted wonderfully and let a shot fly which was just wide of Neto's post.

That was the beginning of a full-on start to the second half which had me on the edge of my settee. This was in stark contrast to what was happening on the TV at Stamford Bridge, enough to send anyone watching to sleep.

Ferguson scooped an effort over the bar whilst leaning back and Joel Veltman raced in and let a shot go. He too was guilty of leaning back with the ball posing more of a threat to the Bournemouth fans behind the goal than Neto.

Pascal Gross put a strike straight down the throat of Neto, who parried for a corner. Brighton were beginning to finish strongly and De Zerbi obviously wanted to maintain the momentum as he made some bold subs, bringing on Julio Enciso and Yasin Ayari.

Enciso was quickly into the game with a first attempt just wide of the left-hand post. It did not take him long to find the back of the net, some great footwork creating space through which he practically walked the ball into the back of the net.

What a first goal in Brighton colours for Julio Enciso. I am certain it will not be his last either, and the togetherness of the squad was shown through the way in which they all wanted to celebrate with their young teammate and the fans at the full-time whistle.

I still have to pinch myself that the Albion are sixth in the Premier League. Aston Villa are chasing us down, but why worry about what is happening below us when we have Spurs in our sights?

Everything is crossed now for a good performance on Saturday.

Incompetent officials overshadowing how good Brighton are.

How do you even begin to describe what we witnessed between Spurs and Brighton on Saturday afternoon?

I was not at the Tottenham Hotspur Stadium myself but listened to the game live on BBC Radio Sussex. I have since watched *Match of the Day* and also the extended highlights on both Sky Sports and the Albion website.

One thing is quite clear above everything else — Brighton are great at football. That is what should be discussed afterwards. The performance of the Albion in outplaying Spurs rather than endless debates about VAR and another set of apologies from

PGMOL (Professional Game Match Officials Ltd) for costing us more goals and lost points.

The incompetence of match officials is overshadowing the best times to be a Brighton fan. When referees are always the talking point rather than players and teams, the Premier League has a serious problem. It makes the claims of it being the best league in the world sometimes laughable.

Brighton had the upper hand over Spurs, only to be undone by a combination of factors not just involving the refereeing team.

Son Heung-min scored a superb out-of-the-ordinary goal and then the Albion left Harry Kane alone to add a second.

One defensive error punished by the England captain cost Brighton a point. And of course, the officials both on and off the pitch have lost them all three points.

There is still though much to play for. Remember what they say, "It is never over until the fat lady sings." Hopefully, Roberto De Zerbi and the lads have not become too disheartened by it all.

Also hopefully, we do not see Stuart Attwell again for some time. I am afraid to say he just does not cut it at this level of football.

Fairness plays a huge part in life and so it should. The law, for example. If something goes to any court and it is deemed to not be fair, it is thrown out because of the European Court of Human Rights.

When things are not fair, then apologies are not enough. In those circumstances, individuals and businesses should be compensated for being impacted by unfair treatment, whether it be deliberate or a mistake.

Should the FA take a similar approach to referee incompetency? Should there be a panel in place to judge whether Saturday's points should be shared between Spurs and Brighton, or even awarded retrospectively to the Albion because of such gross unfairness?

Could the game be replayed because the result was so badly impacted by the officials getting things wrong?

And what about VAR? Lewis Dunk said afterwards what is the point in having it if you do not bother to use it for checking incidents like the two penalties Brighton were denied? The captain is right.

Those operating VAR are clearly not up to the job and cannot cope with the pressure. How can those at Stockley Park watch the foul on Kaoru Mitoma and not give a penalty?

Mr Attwell was pretty close to that incident and managed to miss it. It felt like VAR decided it was not a penalty because it wanted to back Mr Atwell's original decision, which is not the point of the technology. In any case, Mr Attwell should have gone to Specsavers I think.

I have watched the second disallowed goal incident with Danny Welbeck over and over again. Welbeck's shot appeared to hit the thigh of Alexis Mac Allister, who can be seen moving his arm out of the way.

So many contentious decisions went against Brighton, even Lord Sugar tweeted to say the Albion had been treated unfairly.

To make up your own mind about what happened, you have to watch the highlights. Away from all the controversy, you see that Spurs were under real pressure. When this happens, the big clubs always resort to gamesmanship in their desperate quest for points, particularly near the end of the season.

We saw clearly that when Spurs played Everton on Monday night and Harry Kane could have won a Hollywood Oscar for his acting performance in getting Abdoulaye Doucoure sent off.

It happened as well in Liverpool's 2-2 draw with Arsenal. The Trent Alexander-Arnold incident riled the Kop up and the whole match turned from that point in Liverpool's favour as they overcame being 2-0 behind.

During the run-in, to the end of the season, Brighton must not let any opponents get under their skin. Do not take the bait, forget the other team, and forget the officials; our players are better than most.

We will surely see this occur when facing the masters of acting up, Manchester United in the FA Cup semi-finals.

Before that, it is the trip to Frank Lampard's Chelsea next week. Brighton will be hoping to improve on seventh place, having been overtaken now by Aston Villa but we have two games in hand on Villa.

De Zerbi may be missing from the dugout again after he and Spurs' manager Cristian Stellini were shown red cards.

Hopefully, an apology from De Zerbi will suffice to get him

off the hook. Saying sorry with no further punishment is enough for the PGMOL, so why not for our head coach? What is good for the goose is good for the gander I say!

I bet it will not work that way, however. All Brighton can do is keep playing their football and hope that fairness prevails so that their amazing season is not remembered more for refereeing mistakes than anything else.

Bookies favourites Brighton make Chelsea go west for second time.

Did you ever think you would see the day when pundits and bookies would have Brighton marked down as favourites for an away game against Chelsea?

Their faith turned out to be correct, as for the second time this season Chelsea ended up "going west" against the Albion.

The meaning of to go west in English is when something is lost, damaged, or spoiled in some way. Well, Mr Todd Boehly has spoilt the Blues in more ways than one since taking over!

Despite being above Chelsea in the table, Brighton needed to be wary arriving at Stamford Bridge. It was Frank Lampard's first home game back in charge and the Blues would be looking to bounce back from defeat against Real Madrid in the Champions League.

That is the only competition Chelsea have left to play for this season and with the second leg coming up, there was talk that Lampard would rest players against the Albion.

Brighton though are now at a point where it does not matter who we face. The Albion are getting stronger and stronger with each match that they play for Roberto De Zerbi, and so it proved once again with the Seagulls winning a league game away against Chelsea for the first time in their history. How proud are we of our lads?

I have been saving my old age pension for next weekend's trip to Wembley so could not be at Stamford Bridge. The away supporters sounded in fantastic voice over the BBC Radio Sussex airwaves, drowning out the home fans in The Shed. It was brilliant to listen to and hopefully we make as much noise at the FA Cup semi-final at Wembley.

Hopefully, the weather is similar, too. Johnny Cantor and Warren Aspinall informed us it was a sunny, spring day in the capital and Brighton were quick off the mark, not needing long before Evan Ferguson let rip a shot that hit the bar.

There was much to get excited about in that opening 10 minutes. My old settee springs took a bashing and even the dog was getting wound up as well.

But then Chelsea scored, totally against the run of play. Mykhailo Mudryk cut in from the right to the centre and slipped a pass to Conor Gallagher.

His shot unfortunately kicked up off the back of Lewis Dunk's boot. Robert Sanchez was about to move to his left when the deflection took the ball right and that split second was enough to mean the Albion goalkeeper could not quite get to the shot.

The BBC's *Match of the Day* and the Sky Sports highlights did not really show the wealth of chances that Brighton had created.

Had the Albion been more clinical, the equaliser would have arrived long before it did. Finishing is something De Zerbi will have the players working on this week I am sure, along with practicing penalties ready for Sunday just in case!

Brighton also found Kepa Arrizabalaga in the Chelsea goal giving a man-of-the-match performance with a number of great saves throughout the game.

The Albion had to overcome two injury blows before they scored. Trusted right back Joel Veltman left at 28 minutes to be replaced by Julio Enciso.

Just 10 minutes later and Evan Ferguson had to be taken off with Danny Welbeck coming on, following Ferguson landing awkwardly after having a header saved by Kepa.

Let us hope Veltman and Ferguson do not miss out on Wembley next week; both have been excellent this season and deserve the chance to play in an FA Cup semi-final.

Welbeck had only been on the pitch for three minutes when he scored. Pascal Gross crossed and sandwiched between two blue shirts rose the crimson number 18 to nod the ball past Kepa.

The injury curse looked like it might continue when Sanchez did some damage against his own goalpost when saving.

Fortunately, he was okay and that rare attack from Chelsea ended with a Brighton free kick anyway for offside.

BBC Radio Sussex told us that Brighton began the second half playing even better football than in the first. All the Albion needed was a goal.

Brighton were not waiting for Chelsea to make errors but forcing them into doing so. A Kepa attempt to play out from the back was brilliantly intercepted by Moises Caicedo, who worked the ball to Welbeck for a shot straight into the hands of the home goalkeeper.

The Albion were fighting for every ball, quickly pressing Chelsea and catching their sluggish hosts napping on many occasions.

Enciso in particular was playing his heart out. At one point, he skipped past not one but two Chelsea defenders and managed to crack a shot away from a tight angle.

Kepa parried and the rebound fell to Danny Welbeck who put it over the bar. The chance came quickly to Welbeck, making it impossible to control or get the precision needed to score.

But what about Julio Enciso? What a player this lad is. His tenacity, determination, and will to win showed through. I hope he plays at Wembley against Manchester United as he could be the difference maker.

Enciso of course hit the winner in style. Before that though, Sanchez had to pull off a double save from Reece James and Mudryk as Chelsea went on a rare attack.

The Albion's aggression led to their second goal. Joao Felix was harried into losing possession, Solly March cut in from the left and found Enciso in the middle.

Enciso was still a long way from the Chelsea goal but still decided to shoot with his right foot from 30 yards plus. It went with so much pace that slow-motion replays found it had to track the ball as it flew into the top corner.

Even Kepa having one of those games where he seemed to be saving virtually everything had no chance of keeping it out.

Enciso ran straight to the Brighton supporters behind the goal, jumping onto the hoardings and celebrating with his teammates. Everyone knew they had just witnessed something truly special, a proper Goal of the Season contender.

There were still 21 minutes remaining, but Brighton had been so good and Chelsea so abject, you thought at that point it was probably the winning goal.

Brighton maintained their lead despite six minutes of injury time. What a victory for the Albion and the perfect way to go into Wembley, restoring faith and confidence after the disappointment of the controversial defeat at Spurs a week earlier.

Now we look forward to Sunday. In all my years, I have never ever had the opportunity to go to Wembley and I am really looking forward to it. Whether we win or lose it will be a great experience.

Seagull Travel has made the transport side so easy and the club's allocation system seemed to work well, including getting further tickets for those who missed out the first time around.

Whatever the result, days like FA Cup semi-finals are the ones that stay with us forever!

Brighton did us proud — and will be back at Wembley again soon.

From the moment the full-time whistle blew on Chelsea 1-2 Brighton at Stamford Bridge, the anticipation had been building towards the FA Cup semi-final between the Albion and Manchester United at Wembley.

On Tuesday evening, there was the Albion Unlimited podcast on BBC Radio Sussex with Johnny Cantor and Warren Aspinall. On Thursday, Lewis Dunk was interviewed by TalkSport Radio and Glenn Murray interviewed the captain on the Pier for television.

The Premier League might be the most watched in the world, but the media attention the Albion were receiving for the FA Cup was unlike your everyday match.

Compared to United, Roberto De Zerbi enjoyed a smooth week of preparation too. The win against Chelsea left a fantastic mood with everyone now talking about Julio Enciso after his tremendous winner which rifled into the back of the Blues goal.

Joel Veltman and Evan Ferguson had been hit with injuries, but the Albion still had eight days between games. United in contrast played on Thursday night in Spain against Sevilla — or shall we say instead they turned up.

If you watched that game on television, you would have been quietly encouraged going into Wembley because United were poor, well beaten, and out of Europe.

They then appeared to have flown straight back to London, as Erik ten Hag's press conference for the semi-final looked like it was taking place in a makeshift media centre in a hotel.

De Zerbi and his Brighton players were not the only ones preparing for the day. So too were Seagull Travel, who moved hell and high water to get as many fans as they could to Wembley by coach.

The final total was, I believe, 78 coaches on the road. They also arranged at great expense; a reserve coach based at Cobham Services on the M25 in case of a breakdown.

It was a well-oiled machine and the communication with travellers was fantastic. They kept in touch with everyone who booked onboard throughout the day and helped and assisted an injured traveller who fell and cracked his head open, according to their reports.

Our coach from Lindfield in Sussex set out at 11.10 a.m. By 1.15 p.m., we had navigated the M23 and M25 and were pulling into the pink car park at Wembley Stadium.

It was all so easy. No stress, no hassle, and a driver who knew his stuff. From the car park, we walked towards this most iconic of stadiums through what can only be described as nasty drizzle rain.

We had plenty of time to explore. However, the older you get, the more tiring it becomes to get around these huge buildings and complexes. Our entry point was J and we whisked through security and the turnstiles; boy, was I excited now.

As I said last week, I have never been to Wembley before. Work commitments have always prevented it on the five previous times Brighton have visited.

Being a little peckish, I decided to get a burger and chips for my wife and me before it got busy. £27.90. Yes, I nearly had a coronary, for two burgers and chips in a small bun.

Thank the lord for our fabulous fish and chip van at the Amex. The £27.90 burger and chips turned out to be the first of three robberies that occurred on that day.

To make matters worse, it was the most disgusting burger I think I have ever had as well. The staff also looked at me as if I was barmy when I asked for a little salt on my chips.

"We don't have salt," was the reply. The whole burger experience was not a highlight for me. I still don't know if it was worse than robbery number two or robbery number three, which we will get to shortly.

After getting rid of this barely warm, barely cooked burger in a cold bun, I feasted my eyes on some of the incredible outfits Albion fans had turned up wearing.

Nobody could have been in any doubt if they did not already know that Brighton wear blue and white and are called the Seagulls!

I also came across Michaela Norris, who was even more suitably dressed for the occasion. Do we need more people turning up to games at the Amex in full seagull costumes?

Next, it was time to investigate block 136. Walking into that stadium even when it is filling up is something else.

When we got to our position, we discovered the club had gone to the expense of putting a blue or white flag on every seat. The spectacle must have looked fantastic on TV. Thank you, Mr Bloom!

The atmosphere turned out to be electric. 3 p.m. arrived and the national security alert went out on all our mobile phones, thankfully only as a test run, for the first-ever time.

A fascinating afternoon was taking place across the Premier League at the same time. Spurs went 5-0 down at Newcastle in only 20 minutes on their way to losing 6-1, leading to Christian Stellini being given the sack the day after.

Bournemouth lost 4-0 at home to West Ham, leaving us all hoping there would be as many goals and as much entertainment at Wembley.

The prediction I feared the most was BBC correspondent Chris Sutton, who predicted that United would win on penalties after a 2-2 draw.

Sutton was right about the penalties of course, and that was the second robbery of the day. The third robbery was that somebody stole my Brighton FA Cup scarf afterwards.

I dropped it on my seat when leaving and even though I realised before I had reached the end of the aisle and went straight back to my seat, it was gone.

You may have noticed that I have not said much about the football itself. So much has already been written, that I do not want to dwell on it.

Brighton played well. Manchester United played slightly better. For one kick of the game decided the whole show. What a cruel way to lose.

Nonetheless, this being my first time at Wembley meant it was a very special day for me. I was convinced beforehand that whatever the outcome, I would be proud of the Albion.

This turned out to be very much the case; they all played their hearts out and Solly March should not linger on his miss but instead remember all he has achieved in his decade at Brighton.

Mr Paul Barber wrote an open letter the day after the game, saying: "And, as with the successes we've enjoyed together this season, we'll endure yesterday's loss together too — and we'll rally around Solly, who has had a magnificent season so far and is a big reason why we're in this position going into the business end of the season."

"We all need to demonstrate our strength and resilience today, for the rest of this week, and the remainder of the season. There's a lot of football left to play and so much more we can achieve."

"Thank you to everyone — not least our players, Roberto, and his staff — for all the hard work and enjoyment we've shared to date. And thanks to all our staff who worked so hard at Wembley."

"Let's make sure we remain positive and focused, and let's all get ready to go again and support the team at Nottingham Forest on Wednesday and Wolves at the Amex on Saturday. We've got a few big weeks ahead, and your support will be so important".

Mr Barber was right. We must put Wembley firmly behind us and instead focus on three points on the banks of the Trent, followed by giving the players a proper homecoming against Wolves at the Amex the following weekend.

Lewis Dunk channelled his inner Winston Churchill, in a very brave interview immediately after the game at Wembley with BBC Radio Sussex.

Mr Churchill was famous for saying never give up. Brighton will not either, and as Lewis Dunk told listeners, Brighton will definitely be back at Wembley again and fighting for trophies.

We should believe him. Our time is coming, and this is only the start for Brighton and Hove Albion!

Fatigue at Forest never meant the season was over for Brighton.

I know some folks will say that highly paid professional Premier League footballers should be able to cope with playing twice a week. It happens all the time from the Championship down, after all.

What Brighton faced across Wembley and Nottingham Forest away was different. A tough 90 minutes, then 30 minutes of extra time, then penalties, then to lose 7-6 in the shootout and see an FA Cup final place slip through your fingers. All of that was made doubly tough by the Albion being the better team and deserving to beat Manchester United.

Brighton had from 8 p.m. on the Sunday evening after the semi-final until whatever time they set off for Nottingham on Tuesday to recover, with kick-off at the City Ground on Wednesday at 7:30 p.m.

Less than 72 hours to recover and recharge before hitting the road again. Now in my book, that is tough for any athlete. Even more so for the Albion, who have spent this entire season running the extra mile to try and make history for our club.

We all want this history to happen and that is what makes games like Notts Forest hard to take. But it was never going to be a case of season over or Europe out of the question just because of defeat at the City Ground, with eight games still to play, there was everything to play for.

Fatigue affects the thought process as well as the physical performance. The lads deserved to be cut some slack, even more so, if you watched how tired United became in their midweek second half at Spurs.

United were 2-0 up at half time against a Tottenham side supposed to be in crisis. Spurs though got a second wind and it finished 2-2.

Before the 6-0 hammering of Wolves on Saturday, Brighton could collect a maximum of 24 points between losing at Forest and the end of the season on Sunday 28th May.

Three are now in the bag against opponents who had nothing

to play for. United, Everton, and Arsenal are all fighting hard for points for different reasons and will therefore be difficult matches.

Newcastle United though might have already secured a Champions League place when Brighton go to St James' Park. Southampton could be already relegated by the time they visit the Amex and Manchester City crowned champions.

However, if any of those three teams take their feet off the gas, then Brighton will be ready and waiting to pounce. Aston Villa on the final day looks likely to be a tense affair if European qualification goes down to the wire.

It is, however, quite possible the Albion could pick up 15 points or more (always think positive) from the seven games now left and that would surely be enough for the top seven. Forest was nothing more than a blip and an excusable one at that, what with the fatigue issue.

De Zerbi made only three changes at the City Ground. Facundo Buonanotte, Levi Colwill, and Jason Steele came in. The match was broadcast on BT Sport whilst those of us who like to listen to Johnny Cantor and Warren Aspinall had that privilege as normal over the BBC Radio Sussex airwaves.

Nearly 3,000 Brighton fans made the journey to Nottingham with many not getting home until after 3 a.m. due to problems on the roads. Their backing of the Albion deserves to be heavily applauded; they played a part in creating a really intense atmosphere.

From the moment referee Jarred Gillett blew his whistle to kick the game off, it appeared to be a very fast start. Brighton may not have wanted that after their Sunday exploits, but they did soon grow into the game.

Forest possesses a player or two who can take an extremely long throw. Watching the extended highlights on the Albion website, at one point it was like a line out from Twickenham. The Brighton scrummage led by Steele and Lewis Dunk had to hold firm to stop Forest going over for a try.

The Albion made a number of little errors in the opening 10 minutes, which came from bad judgement. When your body is tired, your judgement can be off; those of you who are getting on in years like me will already know this!

It was one such piece of bad judgement that gave Forest an early penalty. Morgan Gibbs-White crossed from the left towards the far post, a pretty pointless cross as there was no home player to pick it up.

Pervis Estupinan gained possession but that turned out to be short-lived. Estupinan dallied, Neco Williams pounced, and the Forest man now had the ball.

Estupinan caught Williams' foot as he tried to recover and with Mr Gillet right there, the referee was quick to point to the spot.

Brennan Johnson now faced Steele. Steele made a superb save, pushing the ball to his right to stop the Albion from going 1-0 behind before the 15-minute mark. Forest then had another cracking shot which shaved the left-hand post.

After surviving that, Brighton began to improve. Kaoru Mitoma did what he does best, racing down the left-hand side to reach the by-line and cut back beautifully to Julio Enciso.

Enciso was in the middle of the goal on the penalty spot. His shot though was too close to Keylor Navas, who tipped over the bar with a strong hand. Perhaps if Enciso had gone low and hard, he would have scored.

To see Mitoma in full flight was to be reminded of what a great job Aaron Wan-Bissaka did for Manchester United in shutting down the threat posed by the Japanese Bullet Train at Wembley.

Another player to shine in the FA Cup semi-final was Lewis Dunk. He was at it again against Forest when Johnson broke clear, only for the Albion captain to chase him down and put him off into shooting wide.

Enciso was into the action again next, weaving his way out of a tight spot breaking down the right, and spotting a pass inside to Solly March.

Despite there being two Forest defenders there, March was able to turn and lay the ball into the path of Alexis Mac Allister. Unfortunately, Mac Allister side-footed wide of the post.

It was debutant Buonanotte who gave Brighton the lead with a poacher's finish. Buonanotte started the move in the centre circle, breaking and passing right to March.

Showing no lack of confidence after Sunday's penalty miss, March went for goal with a brilliant shot on target too hot for Navas to handle. The rebound fell to Buonanotte, showing great awareness to be in the right place at the right time to tap home his first goal for the Albion.

It looked like Brighton were going to make it to half time ahead until Forest struck literally seconds before the whistle with 48 minutes on the clock.

Renan Lodi crossed from the Forest left and the ball hit enough of Pascal Gross' boot to deflect past the off-guard Steele and into the back of the net. The sort of bad luck you do not need when your players are already running on empty.

The goal fired Forest up and you could hear over the radio how rocking the City Ground was. Brighton were not intimidated at first, Estupinan shooting wide followed by Buonanotte breaking free and racing towards goal.

Only Navas was ahead of Buonanotte and one Forest defender closing. Buonanotte showed great awareness to realise he was about to be tackled, playing a square pass unselfishly to Mitoma on his left. Mitoma went for goal but was uncharacteristically off target, the shot going just wide of the opposite post.

The game became more stretched after that and I became increasingly worried Brighton were going to concede. You could see every Forest player was fighting for their club's Premier League survival and the fans too were the definition of a 12th man.

A nasty injury to Williams brought the noise levels down for a moment. Gibbs-White crossed and in the resulting goalmouth scramble, two Forest players collided. Williams was one, stretchered off, and then taken to hospital with what turned out to be a broken jaw. We all wish him a speedy recovery.

Brighton were visibly starting to tire by now and it was an error from Caicedo which saw Forest take the lead again in the 69th minute. Danilo tackled the Albion midfielder, broke forward, and beat Jason Steele. Another minor mistake which Forest to their credit made the Albion pay heavily for.

Colwill was next to give the ball away. Johnson benefitted this time, but luckily his shot was over Steele's crossbar. At this point, it seemed there was only going to be one winner.

March, though, nearly came up trumps by equalising against the run of play with a shot that needed another really good save from Navas, making it two strong stops to counter the spillage for Buonanotte's goal.

Forest responded by going on another powerful break to earn a corner. The set piece was delivered to the penalty spot, where it hit the hand of Dunk after the Brighton captain raised his arms high above his head.

VAR checked and the result was a second Forest penalty. Unlike the first, this one was successfully put in the back of the net by Gibbs-White with 91 minutes played.

That injury to Williams meant there were still nine minutes after that. Brighton though could not find a way back, even as Deniz Undav had a goal disallowed for offside.

The noise which greeted the full-time whistle from the Forest fans as they climbed from the relegation was something else. For Brighton, it was a case of filing it under an evening to forget in difficult circumstances.

Onwards and upwards to Wolves, where fatigue apparently played less of an issue!

De Zerbi showed his intuition and judgement against Wolves.

April 29th is a very special day for me. It is my wedding anniversary. And what better way for my wife and I to celebrate than Brighton putting six goals past Wolverhampton Wanderers at the Amex?

Where do we start? A lovely spring afternoon with the sun shining and blue sky set the scene. I felt it best not to eat too many chips before the game as were off for a meal in the evening, so gobbled down only a small portion.

It was so nice not to have to pay those exorbitant Wembley prices and also be able to have some salt on my chips which the national stadium could not supply, as I mentioned last week.

Roberto De Zerbi opted to rest up his squad after recent exertions in the FA Cup and at Nottingham Forest, making five changes to the starting XI.

I thought this understandable, but many folks were surprised, based on what I heard on arriving at the Amex. So too was Paul Merson on *Soccer Saturday*.

Clips that aired on social media appeared to imply that Merson thought De Zerbi had rested so many players because Brighton do not want to play in Europe unless of course the footage had been doctored to make it appear that is what he was saying.

Oh, ye of little faith. De Zerbi's decision making proved impeccable. What excitement, what skill, and what football the Albion treated us to even with Moises Caicedo, Alexis Mac Allister, and Kaoru Mitoma watching on from the bench.

There are not many teams in the Premier League who could rest three of their most important players and then score six goals. It just goes to show what a special manager we have, with great intuition and judgement.

In any case, subs could have been made if things were not going well for Brighton and Caicedo, Mac Allister and Mitoma brought on.

It became quite clear very quickly, however, that their services would not be needed as a spectacular afternoon kicked into life after only six minutes.

The opening goal began with Julio Enciso driving down the left to find Pervis Estupinan on the overlap. Estupinan crossed to the far post, Solly March retrieved and played back to Joel Veltman.

He hit a ball along the turf for Danny Welbeck, who flicked it into the path of Deniz Undav. It was a great piece of play from Welbeck and Undav calmly put the ball past Wolves goalkeeper Jose Sa. There was a lengthy wait whilst VAR checked to see if Undav was offside. For once, VAR found in the Albion's favour.

It was a relief not to see Brighton undone by an incorrect decision. I always now double check the referee before a game as I dread these poor officials costing Brighton dearly as they have done in this 2022 -2023 season.

We are not the only club of course to suffer. Such mistakes by referees and VAR can be huge with so much at stake.

Take Everton, for example. The Toffees are struggling financially, have a new stadium being built which needs paying for, and fans who are very unhappy.

We are so very lucky at Brighton to have an owner like Mr Tony Bloom and his trusted team under Mr Paul Barber. Long may it continue as we are beginning to really see the fruits of all their labours.

Wolves too have endured a disappointing season and what was to follow after Denis Undav put Brighton ahead must be their worst result of their season.

Historically, a 6-0 win made for Brighton's biggest-ever win in the Premier League. The Albion frequently took possession off Wolves in midfield and were ruthless when they did so, cutting through the visitors like a hot knife through butter.

Goal number two came from Brighton winning the ball and Billy Gilmour finding Julio Enciso. Like a bat out of Paraguay, Enciso sped away down the left flank. What speed he has.

Enciso initially appeared to have gone down a bit of a blind alley, with five Wolves players and Sa around him.

He managed to find the space to expertly cross to the waiting Pascal Gross, who used his left foot to beat Sa and double the lead with 13 minutes played.

Welbeck did actually miss a chance that came from a Lewis Dunk long ball. A Wolves defender passed back to Sa, who in turn miscalculated his own pass to gift the ball straight to Welbeck. Unfortunately, Welbeck lent back as he struck his shot and the ball flew over Sa's head and the crossbar.

Wolves responded to that let off by calling upon Jason Steele to make a great block from Matheus Nunes. It was one of the only chances the visitors created all afternoon.

Goal three came for Brighton in the 26th minute and again, Enciso was involved. Gross started the move, feeding the ball left and then continuing his run towards the edge of the D to receive the ball back from Enciso.

The control from Gross was nothing short of outstanding, letting the ball pop up and then volleying into the top corner for a truly stunning finish.

Not even half an hour had been played by this point and already, I was worn out watching. The Amex crowd were understandably in great spirits and that led to a brilliant atmosphere.

We will need to bring the noise levels again on Thursday evening when Manchester United visit with another three precious points on the line.

Another Wolves mistake from Mario Lemina was pounced upon again by Enciso, who nearly punished the error with a fourth before half time.

Brighton did manage to score again prior to the break. Gilmour went left to Enciso, Estupinan overlapped and crossed towards the back post for Welbeck to casually rise and head past Sa.

There was still time for Solly March to have a go with an attempt just over. Brighton ended the half as they had started it; all over Wolves with no quarter given.

When referee David Coote blew his whistle, it was a much-needed rest to stabilise the blood pressure. Wolves meanwhile had the chance to regroup, which Julen Lopetegui used to make a treble change during the half-time break.

This appeared to make no difference as the Albion scored number five three minutes into part two. Welbeck struck again with a shot from outside the area, giving Sa no chance.

Now I may be wrong, but there were many empty seats appearing in the away end as the game went on and the goals rained in. I think the Wolves fans had started their long journey early, not wanting to face any more humiliation.

Still, Brighton kept attacking, now wanting six. Estupinan came close to his first Brighton goal, a block meaning he has to wait for another day. But it will surely not be long until he opens his account.

Undav was the player who added the sixth on 66 minutes. Mitoma had only just been introduced when he won possession for the Albion, the ball heading right to Undav.

It was a very tight angle made more difficult by Sa bearing down on Undav. Undav expertly chipped the ball so calmly over the head of Sa.

The ball kissed the bar just slightly, dropping down and over the line. A fantastic finish to earn Undav a well-deserved brace and Brighton six goals in the Premier League for the first time.

The excitement was not over yet. Caicedo came on and should have done better with a big chance; nitpicking it might be, but his finishing still needs some work!

Gilmour clipped the right-hand post and Estupinan was tackled and knocked off balance just as he was about to shoot. Six goals could easily have been easily eight, nine, or even ten.

Instead, we had to settle for only six. What a way to bounce back from the two defeats of the previous seven days, putting the second target for the season of a place in Europe back on the table.

Three consecutive home games offer a huge opportunity to move closer to that aim. Three points from Wolves can be followed up with more against United and Everton, especially with the noise and passion Brighton fans provided in the Wolves and Forest games and at Wembley.

Such an exciting time to be an Albion supporter. I wonder what will happen next.

CHAPTER 10
May 2023

Six points from three home games leaves Europe in Brighton hands.

BEFORE BRIGHTON BEGAN their run of three home games against Wolves, Manchester United, and Everton, how many points would you have been happy to see the Albion take?

Despite the 5-1 defeat to the Toffees, we remain in the hunt for European qualification with our fate in our own hands thanks to six points.

Had Brighton beaten Wolves and Everton and lost to United rather than beating United and losing to Everton, would everyone be as downcast?

Probably not, which is why I look at that magical Thursday evening at the Amex, the performance of the Albion, and what pundits and opposition fans said about us as being the real Brighton. Everyone is allowed an off day after all, which is what we saw against those sticky Toffees.

To be a season ticket holder at the Amex watching the Albion play Manchester United was a real privilege. The Sussex coastline had a few early evening light showers, but they cleared before kick-off to leave a lovely late Spring night, perfect for football.

As the sun set before kick-off, it left the packed South Stand of away fans bathed in light. Most of them had probably had an easy journey from London and the south (I would love to know how many true Mancunians were there).

Erik ten Hag walked over to the United fans at 7:15 p.m., 45 minutes before kick-off. He posed for selfies with those in the stands, a nice touch from a man who comes across as a charming Dutchman.

Erik ten Hag warmly greeted Mr Paul Ince, who was part of the Sky Sports pundits team, like a true gentleman. None of that surprised me as I have many good friends in the Netherlands from my days as a firefighter.

Watching the Sky coverage back, Mr Ince appeared to be a worried United supporter. Mr Jamie Redknapp on the other hand had nothing but praise for Brighton, Mr Tony Bloom, and Mr Paul Barber.

Mr Redknapp believed that the Albion would do very well over their remaining matches and that Europe was a very realistic target. It remains that way, even after the Everton game.

Sky also interviewed Mr Barber and Adam Lallana pitch side. This provided a reminder of how lucky we are to have really top people fully behind the scenes and with its best interests at heart, unlike at other clubs we all know that will remain nameless.

Just 24 hours before Brighton 1-0 Manchester United and I had begun to fret a little. Why had there been no smiling press conference from Robert De Zerbi?

I did not know until arriving at the Amex and seeing a tweet from BBC Radio Sussex's Johnny Cantor that Roberto De Zerbi had in fact been ill.

Johnny confirmed that the manager had recovered well enough to be in the dugout at the Amex. De Zerbi would probably be the first to tell you it would have been no problem had he not been there, but I was nonetheless delighted he was present as Brighton looked for revenge against their FA Cup semi-final conquerors.

A family member who is an avid United fan told me he was predicting a 2-1 win for his team. My prediction was 3-1 to the Albion.

We both fancied goals and so how wrong were we! To get through 95 minutes with the scoreline at 0-0 was reminiscent of Wembley.

Most United supporters seem to think they deserved to win that day. Well, that is rubbish, as far as I am concerned. And the same goes for those saying United were robbed on Thursday night.

One on social media said the referee had cost them. My reply to that was you have no idea what that is like. Sit through 90 minutes like Spurs 2-1 Brighton last month and then you will know what a robbery is like.

This same fan went on to claim Kaoru Mitoma should have been sent off after he dived three times to try and win penalties and that Adam Webster deserved a straight red card for a foul on Bruno Fernandes.

They also stated that Luke Shaw was pushed in the back, causing him to handle the ball in the box the way he did. All the evidence, from both video and still pictures, does not show any kind of push.

The only thing this deluded United fan was correct about was that Andre Mariner was poor — but the referee was poor for both sides this time and that meant he did not have a bearing on the result.

United supporters calling up TalkSport radio afterwards were more generous towards Brighton. One said that United played as individuals on the pitch rather than as a team.

He added that if you watch the Albion and the style of play De Zerbi pioneers, every player is in sync and knows what to do. That is why Brighton were able to carve through United like a hot knife through butter on several occasions. As they have with other teams.

The Amex was in great voice before kick-off as the teams emerged, with Moises Caicedo wearing a bodycam as part of a new idea from Sky.

It was a shame Caicedo could not keep it on, to show Mr Mariner the up-close footage of when he got chopped down.

Both sides set their stalls out to attack early. Within one minute and 34 seconds, Anthony had a shot just wide of Jason Steele's left-hand post.

Brighton began to settle with their first chance coming when Mitoma intercepted a poor pass from Victor Lindelof to Aaron Wan-Bissaka.

Mitoma was in on goal but rather than dribbling past David De Gea or squaring to the unmarked Julio Enciso, he shot.

The ball hit the United goalkeeper directly in the face, appearing to knock him flat-out like a light. It took more than five minutes for De Gea to be readied to play again.

Plenty of sparks flew in a hard-fought, end-to-end game. It was scoreless at the break and as the minutes clicked by, I began to worry that United would nick it in the final minutes as they often find a way of doing.

Steele was a huge reason as to why nobody had scored after 90 minutes, making at least four magnificent saves. He has been in wonderful form over recent weeks. De Gea too made some great stops as Brighton tried desperately to find a way through.

And then with the full-time whistle imminent, almost out of nowhere, play was stopped, and Andre Mariner was told by VAR to have a look at a potential handball against Luke Shaw.

Alexis Mac Allister sensibly had the ball already and made sure to stay out of the way of the resulting melee as the United players complained to Mr Mariner after he pointed to the spot.

The stadium appeared to go deathly quiet as Mac Allister stepped up to take the penalty. He placed the ball into the top corner, so coolly and calmly.

With no time left on the clock, the final whistle blew immediately after United had kicked off again. It proved to be the sweetest way possible to beat Manchester United, not just because of what happened 11 days earlier at Wembley but also recalling the time they won at the Amex a few seasons ago with a penalty awarded to them for taking after the full-time whistle had blown.

If Brighton reproduce that footballing performance and fight over the remaining five games, then Everton will remain just a blip.

With our support, the Albion can overcome the setback just as they did after losing at Nottingham Forest.

A bad day at the Amex should not mean a 76th-minute exodus.

Firstly, I want to say how sad I felt for this Brighton squad and Roberto De Zerbi when our supporters started leaving the Amex in their droves when Everton went 4-0 up in the 76th minute of what ended up being a 5-1 defeat for the Albion.

Just because the lads had a bad day at the office, we should not turn our backs on them ever. It was a grotty night weather wise, agreed, and people were understandably wanting to get home at the end of a long bank holiday with many having work the following day.

However, true supporters should stay until the very end. Especially in a season where Brighton have given us so many good memories.

The Albion's efforts in the second half were worthy of appreciation. It was a miles better showing after half time and had it not been for Jordan Pickford and his excellent saves, Brighton might even have caught them up.

De Zerbi has risen expectations such that at the end of a busy weekend of street parties and coronation fever, we are arriving at the Amex expecting to beat Everton and most other opponents.

We must always remember that football is a very strange sport. Surprises happen and things do not always go as you expect. Brighton 1-5 Everton was definitely one of those events.

You would have got amazing odds had you placed a bet that the Albion would concede five goals to the Toffees. The best thing, therefore, is to write it off as a blip on the way towards the ultimate target of Europe.

If at the start of the season, you had been offered a top 10 position again and an FA Cup semi-final, what would you have said? I suspect for most of us it would be yes please, thank you.

So that big target is still possible. Brighton have still only played 33 games, meaning 15 more points are available.

There might be more slip ups like Everton along the way — we all know what the Albion are like. But we also know that the next minute, Brighton are quite capable of producing an amazing, unexpected win against a top-four team.

Which is where we go next, to Arsenal. The pressure will be on the Gunners to get the points as they attempt to win the title. It is a different pressure from the one Everton find themselves under.

The Toffees are fighting for their Premier League lives, which was always going to make them dangerous opponents. There is the added weight of history, with Everton having been a top-flight club since 1955.

Sean Dyche came with a game plan, and it caught out the Albion. It was the sort of plan that Brighton often come unstuck against. We tend to play better against the teams at the top of the table, which again gives us hope going to Arsenal next.

Our journey to the Amex for the Everton game was made using the Seagull Travel coach service from Lindfield. It turned up just ahead of schedule and did sterling work driving us to the ground.

Unlike the Manchester United game last time at the Amex, Monday was far from a lovely spring evening. I purchased my programme and was so pleased to see one of our legends of a bygone era featured.

Mr Warren Aspinall appeared on a double-page spread between pages 24 and 27, outlining his career as a striker. Aspinall played for Everton and the Albion, amongst others.

He made nearly 40 appearances for Brighton towards the end of his career and is of course now one-half of the BBC Radio Sussex Commentary team alongside Johnny Cantor.

Unfortunately, they did not report that Warren is sponsored by Maynard's Wine Gums. I thought this is odd as he tells us over the airwaves, he is partial to the odd wine gum on a regular basis. A man after my own heart.

It was great to see a great photo of Warren and Johnny in the article, all set up to broadcast from a Wembley commentary box position. They both do a fantastic job of keeping those who cannot go to games up to date, sometimes from very difficult and tight commentary positions at away matches. We know Goodison Park is not one of their favourites!

I love the feel of a printed programme, something you cannot get with a digital version. The smell of freshly printed ink reminds me of my days in the publishing arena when I worked for *Golf Illustrated* and *Golf Monthly* and I would get the first printed editions off the press. Long may printed versions continue, I say.

Before the game as a mark of respect to our newly crowned King, we had a rendition of the national anthem. Brighton fans did themselves proud by singing along. Everton fans did not. How disrespectful. Maybe they are all anti-royalists or something?

The falling rain could not dampen any spirits, however. More concerning was Lewis Dunk losing the toss and Everton requesting to change ends.

I thought to myself at the time it was not a good sign. Is that because I am superstitious or crazy? It should not really matter too much which way Brighton kick for 45 minutes, and yet against the Toffees it seemed to have quite the effect.

With the turnaround done, referee Simon Hooper blew his whistle for kick-off. As we know all too well, it took less than 35 seconds for Everton to put themselves in front. Now Brighton were on the back foot.

It looked at the time as if the lads were running with lead boots on. Or maybe they had enjoyed too much pop to celebrate the coronation weekend.

Everton were by far the faster and the quicker team. I am sure De Zerbi will raise energy levels and install the necessary ingredients to ensure a more active approach at Arsenal.

What De Zerbi cannot do, however, is magic back poor old Solly March, Joel Veltman, Adam Lallana, Tariq Lamptey, or even Jakub Moder.

Our injury list is building through having so many fixtures crammed tightly together. We are seeing some tired legs. What this also shows us is that if the bigger target is reached and playing twice a week becomes the norm, the squad will need to be strengthened to cover this.

I am not going to go through each goal and how we conceded it against Everton. So much has already been written about the game.

It is worth mentioning though that the Toffees are no bad team. They beat Arsenal 1-0 in February 2023 and Brentford in March 2023. They have good players and should not be in a relegation battle.

The good news is Brighton get six days rest before facing Arsenal, time to recuperate body and mind and generate some PMA (positive mental attitude).

Our away support will, I am sure, be in great voice at the Emirates and doing all they can to egg the lads onto another way to win.

I will have to take cover in my bunker. My wife and her side of the family are from the Arsenal neck of the woods in London and have been supporting them all their lives.

If we do manage to bring down Arsenal — which is possible, folks — I will be thinking of that famous second world war phrase "Tin hats on everyone" as my life may well not be worth living!

The 2022-23 season has put Brighton on the map like never before.

Sunday 14th May was a fine sunny afternoon and just six days after Brighton had lost 5-1 against Everton at the Amex, the Albion were ready to go again at Arsenal.

A heavy defeat might have a lasting impact on some teams, but not the Albion. Roberto De Zerbi and his trusted coaching team managed to lift spirits and convince the squad that the previous Monday's result was a one-off.

Brighton came into the game clear headed and determined with, as De Zerbi promised, a good mentality to take on the number two team in the Premier League.

The result was a 3-0 victory and as has already been written on the We Are Brighton.Com website after the stunning result, anyone with no knowledge of the table could have been mistaken for thinking the team in blue and white were chasing the title rather than the team in red and white.

What is happening right now at Brighton is not going unnoticed. Local people in Brighton & Hove, East Sussex, and West Sussex know the Albion are putting the city and county they represent on the map by being on the brink of making club history.

Finishing in the top seven will extend the Seagulls name into the European arena of football. In years gone by, I have worked at Gatwick Airport and watched young people arrive in England with their parents, being taken to see Chelsea, Spurs, and the rest.

When I have mentioned the nearest club to Gatwick being Brighton & Hove Albion, just half-hour down the road, many of them had no idea the Seagulls existed.

You can guarantee that is now changing through results like Arsenal 0-3 Brighton and the prospect of playing in Europe. The 2022-23 season has turned the Albion into a club with a worldwide profile and that is a great and wonderful achievement.

Arsenal of course already have that reach. My wife's side of the family are all born-and-bred Gunners, coming from that area of North London. Not me; I am proud to be a product of Brighton & Hove. This conflict in the home meant I had to tread carefully in the hours following the full-time whistle. Only when my wife was out walking the dog did I dare to watch the highlights back; I have to eat, remember!

So being able to write about what happened at the Emirates gives me a sense of relief. Finally, I can talk about the fantastic football played by our great players under the guidance of our brilliant manager.

News filtered through before kick-off that Manchester City had won 3-0 at Everton, upping the pressure on Arsenal. The Gunners had to win to keep pace with City in the title race.

That is probably what made the first half a little bit *Little Britain* for those who remember the sketch, "bitty". One could almost say "feisty". Gabriel Martinelli set the tone early when he felt like taking out Kaoru Mitoma with a forearm smash to the face, sending Mitoma to the ground like a sack of spuds.

Martinelli did not last much longer after that, having to be substituted after a heavy challenge with Moises Caicedo.

Caicedo and Mitoma gave each other a fist pump afterwards, suggesting it was revenge for Martinelli's actions against the Japanese Bullet Train.

Between those two incidents, we saw Julio Enciso receive a long ball from Pascal Gross following a Jason Steele pass nearly intercepted by Gabriel Jesus.

Fortunately, Jesus missed the interception and it led to Enciso beating Ben White and seeing Aaron Ramsdale make a good save with his hand for a corner.

Martin Odegaard tried one of his powerful grass-cutting fizzers which he has scored a few goals from, only for it to speed past Steele's left-hand post.

Jesus then threatened down the right, drilling a similar ball towards goal which had caused Steele to deflect into his own net against Everton. This time, Steele got his foot in the right place and turned the shot past the post.

Mikel Arteta chose a familiar face in Leandro Trossard to replace Martinelli. Trossard almost made an instant impact, collecting a Granit Xhaka pass and letting a shot go from just inside the area which glanced the top of the crossbar.

A tactical adjustment saw Mitoma switch from right wing to left and that led to things really heating up. Mitoma confused White so much that it appeared our former defender was doing the "Hokey Cokey".

Mitoma slipped away whilst White was dancing, dropping a shoulder and hitting a pass back from the by-line through a group of players.

It arrived perfectly at the feet of Enciso, who blasted over when all it needed was a side foot into the onion bag. A lesson to learn for the youngster.

Evan Ferguson was next to go close with a shot just wide after Levi Colwill did really well to keep the ball in play and hook it long up the right channel.

Bukayo Saka flashed off an effort of his own equally close as the first 45 minutes finished goalless. I headed off to put the kettle on and keep a low profile, knowing at this point that a draw was a much better result for the Albion than Arsenal.

I wondered what the managers had said to their players at half time, For De Zerbi, maybe a case of keep it up and add a touch of calmness in front of goal. If Brighton had been decisive rather than snatching at their chances, they could have taken the lead on a couple of occasions.

Well, it took only six minutes for a cool head to appear in the Arsenal box. Pervis Estupinan chipped a cross after his first attempt had been blocked and Julio Enciso was on hand to nod past Ramsdale with such ease. De Zerbi went mad we saw on the highlights, which was more than I could do in my living room, because of the other side of the family taking Umbridge.

The Gunners responded by going on the search for an equaliser. Reiss Nelson had a shot which again went wide and Trossard forced Steele into a good save.

Arsenal have been top of the Premier League for the majority of this season for a reason and I worried we were about to be shown why.

Brighton though regained some control. A rocket from Alexis Mac Allister zipped not far away before the moment that won the game for Brighton.

This goal was one that no Arsenal player, manager, or fan would have wanted to see. Ramsdale and Trossard had a misjudgement. Pascal Gross pounced, and the ball rebounded forward into space where the onside Deniz Undav was lurking.

Ramsdale charged out and jumped 12 feet into the air to try and put Undav off. Undav was not to be distracted, cleverly lobbing the ball over Ramsdale and into the back of the net.

The Brighton fans went berserk and De Zerbi again showed his passion. There were just four minutes of normal time left and the Gunners knew that was that.

Brighton were not yet done, however. The icing on the cake came when Danny Welbeck did well down the right side to control the ball, keep possession and flick onto Denis Undav.Ramsdale parried Undav's shot but only straight into the path of Pervis Estupinan who controlled his finish to make it 3-0 in the 96th minute.

Arsenal had been beaten by the better team, in the words of my stepson, a real compliment coming from an ardent Gunner whose team's season now appears over.

If you look at what Arsenal has achieved this season, they

should be applauded rather than scolded for all their hard efforts.

Nobody thought they would be in a title race with City, just like not many people expected Brighton to be on the verge of European football.

Three big games remain at Newcastle United, home to Southampton and then away to Aston Villa. Recently relegated Saints is the one game I am not sure about, the way things have been going when you compare the Everton and Arsenal games. Maybe a good showing though would convince James Ward-Prowse to sign on the dotted line?

We will need new players for any European football, after all, to help those who we have to thank for this fantastic season so far.

De Zerbi deserves praise for his careful juggling of the Brighton squad.

The visit to St James' Park to face Newcastle United last Thursday evening was the 11th game Brighton had played since the start of April.

This intense schedule will finish with 14 matches in eight weeks once the Albion have travelled to Aston Villa on the final weekend of the Premier League, after which they can have a well-earned rest.

Up to eight players have been on the injury list at any one time because of the number of games. Such a run would be tough for any team in the Premier League, let alone one with a modest budget like Brighton and lacking the squad depth which bigger clubs can afford to build.

Roberto De Zerbi has been made to carefully juggle his squad, targeting specific games over others to win points. With Brighton now qualified for Europe, we can say he has done so very successfully.

Losing at Nottingham Forest was followed by six points from games against Wolves and Manchester United. After the 5-1 defeat at the Amex to Everton came a 3-0 win at Arsenal.

Those dedicated fans who travelled the nearly 800-mile round trip to Newcastle were given a disappointing evening as De Zerbi rested players again.

All is well that ends well and the rotation meant the Albion were refreshed and ready to beat recently relegated Southampton and achieve a top-six finish.

We all know as Brighton supporters that the Albion over the years never normally manage to achieve their targets the easy way.

Those setbacks against Forest, the Toffees, and the Magpies were maybe to be expected, even without De Zerbi resting players and tiredness being such a factor.

I must admit that the Albion going to Newcastle, I felt the momentum from such a brilliant win at the Emirates Stadium against Arsenal would carry on and lead to Brighton coming out all guns blazing.

That was not to be, and the Albion were definitely not at their best by a long chalk, especially in the first half. The four changes De Zerbi made took their toll.

But when you then see Alexis Mac Allister, Levi Colwill, and Evan Ferguson playing so well against Southampton, you see De Zerbi has the bigger picture in mind. In RDZ we rightly trust.

The Albion came under tremendous pressure early on and Lewis Dunk had an amazing clearance off the line to keep the scoreline at 0-0. Dunk then had to step up to the plate again and make a great block from a Joe Linton cross.

Giving away set pieces when playing Newcastle is always a risky game, as Brighton found out when falling 1-0 behind. The corner maestro Kieran Trippier whipped an in-swinger into the box which Deniz Undav headed backwards.

That is rarely a good thing to do and, on this occasion, the ball ended up in the back of the Albion net. 22 minutes played and Newcastle led 1-0. By way of a Denis Undav own goal.

Plenty more action at the Albion defensive end of the pitch followed. The Magpies ended the game having taken 22 shots, nine of which were on target. Brighton in contrast managed just eight efforts all evening with only two on target.

Eddie Howe had clearly devised a game plan to take on Brighton which his players carried out very well. Newcastle were much more aggressive than they had been when I watched them draw 2-2 with Leeds, putting the Albion under a lot of pressure.

Dan Burn made it 2-0 to Newcastle right at the end of the first half. Undav gave away a foul, Trippier delivered another great set piece and Burn rose tallest to put a header beyond Jason Steele.

The second half did at least bring Brighton supporters some

hope as a more positive display began to put the Magpies on the back foot.

First, though, Jason Steele had to prevent Miguel Almiron from scoring a third for Newcastle with an amazing save. Inspired by that, Billy Gilmour hit an exquisite pass through the middle for Undav. He took the ball sweetly and had no trouble putting it beyond Nick Pope to make it 2-1.

I am sure most of us thought at this point that the comeback was on. However, playing the sort of football Brighton do under De Zerbi always leaves things open for the opposition on the counter-attack.

That is exactly what happened not once, but twice in the space of three minutes. Callum Wilson made it 3-1, then Bruno Guimaraes 4-1 as the Albion suffered another heavy defeat at Newcastle.

You would have taken losing at Newcastle in exchange for three points from Southampton and guaranteed European football next season though, right?

Thanks to Roberto De Zerbi and his juggling, that is exactly what we have. History made.

The sound of Sussex by the Sea as Brighton marched into Europe.

Sunday afternoon arrived, Brighton was bathed in sunshine for a little while and history was made at the Amex with the Albion qualifying for European competition for the first time in their history.

As the commentator on Albion TV put it in the clearest possible terms: "26 years after nearly dropping out of the Football League altogether, Brighton know that if they secure three points today, they will qualify for Europe for the first time ever."

Albion 3-1 Southampton meant it was target achieved. Roberto De Zerbi had guided them every step of the way, and long may that continue. He and this group of players will forever be remembered for doing something nobody else has previously managed in over 120 years of the club's history.

Qualifying for Europe led me to do some reading on our club's great history, which can be found on the official Albion website. Did you know that it was in 1910 that the club adopted the rousing march of "Sussex by the Sea" as its anthem? Now it will be heard all around the continent next season hopefully.

Before the game, it was performed outside the stadium by the North Carolina Marching Band for all fans arriving one hour and a half early to enjoy their performance.

This was then followed by some of the 200 band members coming into the Amex and performing at the pitch side. It was quite the spectacle and certainly helped get the crowd going, to the point I was convinced that "Sussex by the Sea" sounded louder as we sang when the players came out of the tunnel.

The band were not the only welcome guests before kick-off. We were also privileged to see two very brave young lads who have been suffering from Acute Lymphoblastic Leukaemia.

They have been raising thousands of pounds themselves as they have grown stronger for the Royal Manchester Children's Hospital by setting up a challenge of running one kilometre around every EFL and Premier League ground to raise money for this wonderful charity.

What terrific lads they were, bravely trotting around the edge of the stadium as the teams warmed up. Brighton and Southampton players and supporters stood and applauded their efforts.

You could also see the lads stopping on their way to pick up paper money fans had thrown towards them. . . not quite the cashless stadium the Albion would like us to believe the Amex is!

This begs the question, if we wanted to give at the Amex to more great causes like this, we need locations on-site where you can tap your card to donate. How is that for an idea? Well done, lads; keep up the great work!

Southampton had been relegated the previous weekend but that did not stop them from really worrying the Albion on several occasions, even when Brighton were 2-0 ahead.

De Zerbi said that the Saints had to be taken seriously and he was right. He also said afterwards that whilst victory looks 99 percent certain to have secured Europa League, it is not yet mathematically confirmed.

Our head coach wants that one more point from the final two games to guarantee League rather than Europa Conference. Aston Villa could yet pip the Albion to sixth with victory when the sides meet at Villa Park on Sunday and a 16-goal swing.

A 12-0 defeat against Manchester City on Wednesday followed by a 5-0 loss to Villa and it would be seventh place for Brighton! Stranger things (might) have happened.

City beat Chelsea 1-0 in the late Sunday kick-off. Someone mentioned to me that the City bench alone cost £500 million, without even taking into account those in the starting XI.

When you see numbers like that, you realise how well Brighton have done under De Zerbi, Mr Tony Bloom, Mr Paul Barber, and the excellent team around them to break into the top six this season. How they intend to build on this season will be fascinating to witness.

De Zerbi has talked about needing more squad depth and he made five changes from the side who were beaten 4-1 at Newcastle just 72 hours earlier.

Brighton were back to as fuller strength XI as De Zerbi could field at the moment, the manager was working wonders with his squad rotation to get the Albion through such a tough schedule of 14 matches in eight weeks to round off the season.

Kaoru Mitoma had the first chance of the game when shooting wide in seven minutes. Mitoma was clearly frustrated with himself for missing that good opportunity.

Moises Caicedo went close next with an effort saved by Saints goalkeeper Alex McCarthy. Southampton showed they posed a threat when Theo Walcott created an opportunity in the 16th minute. From my position in the East Upper, I assumed the worst. Thankfully, Walcott's good work was wasted by teammate Carlos Alcaraz firing well wide of Jason Steele's left-hand post. We got away with one there.

Almost as bad as that Alcaraz miss was Southampton dropping a clanger and losing possession on the edge of their area.

Mitoma now had only McCarthy to beat but he placed his shot against the post, from where it bounced back into the arms of the grateful Saints goalkeeper to gather safely.

McCarthy was finally beaten in 29 minutes. Alexis Mac Allister fed Evan Ferguson, whose powerful low drive beat a defender and went straight through McCarthy.

Five goals in the Premier League now this season for Evan Ferguson, who is not even 19 years old yet. What a superstar the Albion have on their hands.

Taking the lead seemed to settle Brighton down and Southampton struggled to respond. Walcott did his best with an outside-of-the-boot effort a long way wide to cheers from the North Stand.

The Saints supporters had mellowed somewhat after the opening goal, looking confused as the Albion sang "When the Saints go marching down" towards the South Stand.

A little below the belt, perhaps. It took Southampton seven years to make it back to the Premier League after their last relegation. I wonder how they will fair next season back in the Championship?

Mitoma made up for those two earlier misses by doing what he does best, breaking at high speed towards an opposition defence.

The Japanese Bullet Train brushed past Romeo Lavia, who went to the ground. Referee Paul Tierney rightly waved played on, Mitoma flicked the ball with the outside of his right foot across to Ferguson to slam home his second of the day.

A great finish from Ferguson after great approach play by Mitoma. Brighton led 2-0 five minutes before half time and once a VAR check was completed, we could all relax now. Right?

Wrong! we all know how good James Ward-Prowse is at free kicks, penalties, corners, and generally all-set pieces. That is why Gareth Southgate has him in the England Squad.

Southampton started the second half strongly and in the 58th minute, earned a corner. I said to my wife I thought Ward-Prowse would probably score direct from the corner here. She didn't believe me.

The lady sitting on the other side of me, however, seemed to appreciate the danger and put her head in her hands as Ward-Prowse delivered.

It did appear to be heading straight in before a glancing blow off the head of Southampton defender Mohamed Elyounoussi confirmed it. Brighton 2-1 Southampton.

Four minutes later and Walcott broke down the right following a perfect pass from, guess who, Ward-Prowse. It was reminiscent of the two goals Newcastle had scored in injury time on Thursday night.

Walcott put the ball in the back of the net and the scoreline looked like it had become 2-2. That was until VAR had a look and Walcott was found to be just offside.

Brighton fans rejoiced but none of this was particularly good for the blood pressure. It is a good job my GP sits in the West Stand rather than the East, otherwise he might have spotted me stressing and told me to go home!

Would there be any further action, I wondered? Southampton seemed disheartened by the offside and rather than trying to find another equaliser, they seemed more determined to add to their yellow card count.

It already stood at five when James Bree took out Mitoma, giving Brighton a set-piece opportunity of their own. Pascal Gross delivered straight onto the head of Joel Veltman, denied a fantastic goal only by a strong save from McCarthy.

The Albion put their next set piece to good use. A corner was deflected to the right side of the penalty area for Gross to work some magic. He dummied, chopped back onto his left foot, and threaded a shot through the eye of a needle to beat McCarthy.

Brighton's saint had scored against the Saints. The Albion led 3-1 with 20 minutes or so left and that was surely that.

Mac Allister rocketed a shot just above the bar in the 84th minute but Brighton did not need another goal. Albion easily navigated seven minutes of injury time before the full-time whistle blew.

It was a privilege to be at the Amex, witnessing this amazing day, and being part of the celebrations. I must say they were very moving.

The club had decided to send the players on a lap of honour, so that our younger fans could show their appreciation on a Sunday afternoon rather than at 10 p.m. on a school night, as would have been the case if it happened after the City game on Wednesday.

All the players and their families walked around the pitch to tumultuous applause and thanks from the supporters. it was so lovely to see and really goes to show what a family-based club the Albion is.

It was also marvellous to witness our chairman Mr Bloom and his family celebrating along with CEO Mr Barber, who has been voted this year the Premier League CEO Of The Year. Many congratulations to him.

A special mention to Darren Gallis of Seagull Travel, who also delayed the departure of all the coaches so nobody had to miss out on the celebrations in the stadium after the game had concluded.

Mr Gallis and his team will now have European trips to plan, along with getting fans to home and away games in the Premier League next season.

Get your passports sorted folks. The sound of "Sussex by the Sea" is coming to Europe next season.

The relationship between Bloom and De Zerbi has Brighton thriving.

A nice sunny Wednesday evening in late May was extremely inviting for us all to attend the Amex for the final Brighton home game of the 2022-23 season.

The Albion had already guaranteed a place in the Europa Conference League but that was not enough for Roberto De Zerbi; our trusted coach wanted a top-six finish and Europa League football. It had been De Zerbi and the squad's big target for some time.

A draw against champions Manchester City would be enough. On arrival, it was an odd atmosphere. Some fans were expecting a hammer blow from City and a cropping of our goal difference.

Others felt Brighton would hold their own, helped by City having upcoming FA Cup and Champions League finals. Maybe they would even be hungover from going out on the lash on Sunday night to celebrate their title win.

That was the excuse Pep Guardiola used after the game finished Brighton 1-1 City. Guardiola said that his players had drunk all the alcohol in Manchester, which was a little different from the brilliant interview we saw De Zerbi give Sky Sports alongside Mr Tony Bloom.

It was amazing to watch the harmony and togetherness between the owner and head coach. They respect each other immensely and that relationship has helped Brighton thrive this season. Long may it continue because it feels like the Albion could reach even greater heights.

Earlier in the day and we heard the great news that Lewis Dunk had been recalled to the England squad for games against Malta and North Macedonia.

It may be nearly five years since he last played for his country, but better late than never for Gareth Southgate to acknowledge our captain.

To all of our surprise, De Zerbi reacted by resting Dunk for the City game. There was no Adam Webster either, leaving Levi Colwill and Jan Paul van Hecke the hefty task of dealing with Erling Haaland.

Brighton gave a guard of honour to City before the kick-off, which meant Sussex by the Sea was played with the teams on the pitch rather than whilst walking out.

For me, this is a much better way of doing it, just like how Liverpool play "You'll Never Walk Alone" right before the kick-off to rouse the crowd before the first whistle.

Guardiola and De Zerbi embraced each other on the touchline, two coaches with the greatest admiration and respect for each other. It would seem that Mr Bloom is not the only big fan of De Zerbi.

Phil Foden did not take long to weave his way around Billy Gilmour and Van Hecke, producing a chipped cross to the far post where the giant figure of Haaland loomed. It was a real shock to all of us when Haaland headed the ball over, a very lucky escape for the Albion.

Brighton came back with some great football through the City lines which gave Danny Welbeck a sight of goal. Foden though intercepted, showing what a good player, he is at both ends of the pitch.

Stefan Ortega saved from Gilmour and the champions were starting to realise this might not be the normal procession they are used to.

Ilkay Gundogan fouled Gilmour five yards outside the City box. Welbeck took the free kick, curling up and over the wall and against the crossbar. So close to perfection for Welbeck.

Foden broke again and played in Haaland, who this time broke away from Van Hecke to bear down on Jason Steele. This is it, I thought. However, Steele dived at the feet of the Premier League's lead scorer to make a brilliant save.

That Foden and Haaland link-up play did eventually give City the lead in the 25th minute. Haaland went clear once more but this time he had support from Foden.

A square pass took Steele out of the game and Foden put the ball into the back of the net despite Van Hecke desperately trying to prevent it from crossing the line.

It was a class move by City, though nothing we have not seen

Brighton perform many times this season. The question now was would this become a goal bonanza for the champions?

No, it would not. A deflected shot from Julio Enciso won a corner. Pascal Gross delivered a well-placed ball to Welbeck for a downwards header towards Kaoru Mitoma.

Mitoma dived to force the ball over the line. Unfortunately, he stretched his arms out in front as he went to ground, and the ball got caught up in his hands.

Appeals for handball went up from at least four City defenders. Referee Simon Hooper took no time in awarding a free kick, meaning the goal was disallowed.

Facundo Buonanotte dribbled his way past two City players to crack a shot away, requiring Ortega to produce a great save.

Brighton were now starting to go from one terrific move to another. Colwill moved the ball down the left to Enciso, who took no time to steady himself.

Still being 32 yards out, Enciso hit what can only be described as a laser-guided shot to the very top right-hand corner of the City goal. No goalkeeper in the world could have kept it out. You could tell how good the strike was by the City supporters in the slow-motion replay, mouths wide open in amazement.

One fan even starts clapping before the ball hits the back of the net. This of course was not the first time Enciso has produced a wonder goal, his strike against Chelsea last month was almost as spectacular.

I wondered what the City players thought when Enciso's shot went in. Things nearly became worse for them when Welbeck beat Ortega, only to have strayed a fraction offside when collecting a Mitoma pass. What might have been had that goal stood?

Moments before half time and Foden nearly put City back into the lead with a header across the goal which kissed the top side of Steele's crossbar.

As the second half began, I thought to myself that City would come out all guns blazing. Brighton had been brilliant in the first 45 minutes and the football was so entertaining. What though if City stepped it up?

The Albion never let that happen. Whatever De Zerbi said during his team talk worked and City actually had fewer chances.

Evan Ferguson replaced Welbeck and his first shot needed

to be saved by Ortega. Pervis Estupinan let rip a howitzer of an effort from a similar sort of distance as Enciso in the first half, only for it to be no more than an inch away.

The excitement and speed of the game were almost exhausting. How was I going to be able to teach at 9 a.m. the following morning, and be at it all day?

City substitute Cole Palmer managed to get away down the left to deliver a deep cross. Guess who was waiting at the back post?

Yes, the Jolly Giant of City Haaland. He finally managed to beat Steele, only for a VAR check to take place for a foul by Haaland on Colwill. Mr Hooper had no doubt that Colwill's shirt had been tugged and the goal was chalked off.

One final chance went the way of Brighton. A charge forward left Moises Caicedo with options left, right, and centre. He played it nicely out towards Gross, whose cross into the middle was headed just over by Mitoma.

The full-time whistle brought appreciation from everyone about what we had just witnessed. Not only that but Europa League football was now guaranteed for Brighton.

Mixed in with the celebrations and happiness was a tinge of sadness that this was the last time we might see Alexis Mac Allister, Moises Caicedo, and maybe other top Albion players at the Amex in a Brighton shirt.

Who knows if the opportunity of playing in the Europa League for Brighton might tempt some to stay? It is important to remember that the career of a footballer is short, and they never know what is around the corner Players have to do what they feel is right for them.

Whatever happens, we can be confident that the show will go on. With Mr Paul Barber, Mr Bloom, and Signor De Zerbi at the helm, it is onwards and upwards.

This was the Seagulls Greatest Ever Season. . . again.

When Brighton did so well in the 2021-22 season, I decided to write my first-ever book and self-publish via Amazon.

This went well and it has been available online since last June, as well as the Amex Superstore selling out their small stock of copies within a couple of weeks before Christmas.

The title of the book is *The Seagulls Best Ever Season*. This seemed perfect; we all remember what it felt like to watch the Albion finish in their highest-ever league position of ninth, without having to worry about the possibility of being relegated.

One year on and it turns out that title was not wise. Because now Roberto De Zerbi has led the Seagulls to an even greater season. Sixth place and Europa League qualification for the first time was an effort that made us all so proud of De Zerbi and the players — and made my previous book title untrue.

The Albion being guaranteed sixth place before their visit to Villa Park for the final game of the season meant there was little to play for other than improving the final points tally.

Aston Villa in contrast had to win the game to ensure a place in the Europa Conference League. One therefore expected they would be going hell for leather to keep Spurs out of seventh spot.

As an OAP, I cannot afford to go to all of Brighton's games and so it is Johnny Cantor and Warren Aspinall on BBC Radio Sussex whom I rely upon for commentary whilst watching the live pictures supplied by Sky Sports when the games are broadcast.

There was a bit of a delay in Sky starting their coverage from Villa Park as the League Two playoff final between Carlisle United and Stockport County went onto penalties.

That meant there was no build-up to Villa against Brighton. Whilst us fans at home were almost thrown straight into the action, those at Villa Park were rewarded for following the Albion far and wide with a free blue t-shirt.

On the front it read "RDZ Blue & White Army" and on the back were all the season's away fixtures listed. What a great gesture from the club that was for our fantastic away supporters.

Signor De Zerbi made six changes to the starting XI who had drawn 1-1 with Premier League champions Manchester City on Wednesday night — a game I would go so far as to say Brighton deserved to win.

The most interesting selection was Yasin Ayari, who made his first Premier League start on what was another bright sunny afternoon in Birmingham. There is a song in there somewhere.. . oh yes, The Kinks 1966. That shows my age, I think.

Both teams entered the pitch to a display of claret and blue colour around the ground and plumes of fire from the sidelines.

Villa Park was really hotting up in expectation of a win for Unai Emery's side.

From the moment referee David Coote blew his whistle, the Villans were off. I would call it a twitchy start from the Albion as Villa went in all guns blazing, giving Brighton no chance to settle down.

Jacob Ramsey looked very dangerous down the Villa left. He put in an early cross, finding Leon Bailey for a shot that hit the crossbar. Levi Colwill was alert to clear the rebound and further danger was averted.

It did not take long after that for the hosts to take the lead. Just eight minutes had been played when Ramsey did well again on the left to cut back a pass to Douglas Luiz. In a very composed manner, Luiz slotted past Jason Steele.

Alexis Mac Allister tried to get Brighton immediately back into the game. His brilliant pass slid right through the middle of the Villa defence to put Evan Ferguson away at speed.

Ferguson normally buries such opportunities but alas, it was not to be on this occasion. He got underneath the ball a little too much and it flew over the top of Emiliano Martinez's goal.

Brighton were showing that they were not going to lie down. Julio Enciso delivered a dangerous cross into the area and Deniz Undav beat Martinez to the ball, turning it over the line.

I was up and out of my seat, those settee springs suffering one last Sunday afternoon bashing of the season. But then the VAR box appeared and Enciso was found to be fractionally offside in the build-up. The goal was disallowed, and the score remained 1-0 to Villa.

The 26th minute saw Mac Allister a little too slow on the ball in midfield. He was dispossessed by John McGinn in what looked to me to be a clear foul.

This led to Villa's second goal, a slick and fast move in which Ramsey left Adam Webster behind and squared to Ollie Watkins for a simple tap in past the stranded Steele.

Villa must have thought they were cruising into the Europa Conference League at that point, but Brighton again rallied after conceding.

Joel Veltman squared to Undav, who played a perfect through ball for Ferguson. Again though, Ferguson could not finish the one-on-one as this time a Villa defender just got a touch to divert the shot behind for a corner.

The corner led to Pascal Gross receiving the ball. He turned left and right, looking around but could not find a blue and white shirt.

Villa were swarming everywhere to prevent the Albion from getting a foothold back in the game. It became a little feisty with both sides picking up four yellow cards; a high total for Brighton, who rarely enter the book so much.

Tyrone Mings chopped down Facundo Buonanotte like a sugar cane and that gave the Albion a free kick just inside the Villa half.

Faithful Gross sent the ball into the box and right on the money, Undav brought it under control so skilfully, using his shoulder before twisting and turning the opposite way to the defender. He then fired left footed into the back of the net.

The celebrations were short-lived. . . or so we thought. The linesman had his flag up for offside but when VAR checked, it was revealed that Undav was actually a whisker onside.

Brighton had one back and VAR had actually worked in the Albion's favour, for once. The remaining seven minutes of the first half saw the Albion go on the hunt for an equaliser.

Another chance came to Undav, who this time shot at Martinez. It felt like Villa were holding on for the break with the momentum totally switching after Brighton scored.

The second half petered out somewhat as the hosts did all they could to hold on. Mac Allister nearly fired home following a fantastic cross from Pervis Estupinan.

A misplaced pass from Jason Steele then set up Ramsey for an open goal. It was a surprise to see Ramsey miss such an easy chance, what with the afternoon he had been having up to that point.

And so, the season finished with a 2-1 defeat, but hey, who cares, we are going to play in the Europa League next season. Villa too achieved their goal, so all in all it was a fair afternoon in Birmingham for both sides.

Will we need *The Seagulls Best Ever Season Volume 3* to come May 2024? We will have to wait and see. Up The Albion!

Tony Noble.

CHAPTER 11
The Magic of Sig.Roberto De Zerbi
By Scott McCarthy

THE THING I love about Tony Noble and his words about the Albion is that he is always so positive. Conventional wisdom and watching Victor Meldrew in *One Foot of the Grave* tell us you are supposed to become grumpier with age. Not Tony, who must be the most glass-half-full OAP in the United Kingdom. Unless of course, he cannot get salt to go with his chips at Wembley Stadium.

Take the 2021-22 season, for example. Yes, Brighton finished in ninth place, but the middle of February through to the beginning of April was grim. Six defeats in a row followed by a 0-0 home draw against rock-bottom Norwich City.

The Albion scored just once in those seven matches, Lewis Dunk converting a Pascal Gross free kick for a consolation goal in a 2-1 loss away against Newcastle United. At the Amex, Brighton went over three months without scoring a goal.

From Adam Webster equalising past Chelsea on January 18th until Danny Welbeck finding the net after two minutes against Southampton on April 24th, the home faithful had precious little to cheer. Actually, precious little is being generous. Nothing would be more accurate.

Even amongst tzhat most barren of spells, Tony remained upbeat. His faith was unwavering at a time when deep cleaning the oven offered greater entertainment than heading to the Amex. Before that Norwich game, I even considered giving the Albion a miss because a trip to everyone's favourite Swedish flatpack furniture megastore was more appealing.

This desire to see the absolute best is undoubtedly useful when writing *The Seagulls Best Ever Season*. The clue is in the title, I suppose. Or, as you now have in your hands or on your Kindle (other eBooks are available), *The Seagulls Best Ever Season - 2022-23.*

But I think to truly appreciate the achievements of Brighton in delivering a sixth-place finish and thus book, you have to consider the fact 2022-23 could have gone wrong for the Albion. Very wrong.

I am of course referring to 18 days in September 2022 which, when Brighton fans of the future look back on the history of the Albion in 100 years, will be considered amongst the most important. Those 18 days elevated the Seagulls to previously unchartered heights and whilst the benefit of hindsight means everyone can shrug their shoulders and laugh at what happened, at the time the sense of worry was very real.

Brighton were sitting fourth in the Premier League having just scored five goals in a top-flight game for the first time. After three-and-a-half seasons of hit-and-miss results, things finally seemed to have clicked for the Albion under Graham Potter. And then Potter left.

Tony being Tony, he was far more generous with his take on Potter's departure for Chelsea than most Brighton fans. And Tony was probably right. As he says elsewhere in this book, how many of us would turn down the chance to earn £12 million a year, totalling a potential £60 million over the course of a five-year deal?

The timing was more of an issue, along with Potter taking five members of the coaching staff with him. The Premier League season was only five games old, and the transfer window had shut only nine days earlier.

Had Potter left Brighton in the summer, giving his replacement the opportunity to shape and mould a squad via new recruits as he saw fit, then perhaps the vitriol that came the way of the new Chelsea head coach as he swapped Sussex for West London would have been lessened.

Especially as Potter had been adamant the Albion did not need to sign a new striker. He might have been happy working with only two out-and-out centre forwards in Danny Welbeck and Deniz Undav. But would another manager have willingly chosen to embark on the first half of the campaign with such scarcity?

The general consensus in the footballing world at the time Potter left was that he was the reason Brighton had finished ninth in 2021-22 and begun 2022-23 in such fine form. A lot of Seagulls supporters believed that too.

In which case, it was an obvious conclusion to draw that the Albion would start sliding down the table without Potter. How far was the question? Aspirations of Europe which Potter had fuelled seemed certain to be dashed. A top 10 finish looked unlikely. Might the Albion even get sucked into a relegation battle, making the previous year's ninth spot nothing more than a brief flirtation with the upper half of the Premier League?

So yes, at the point Potter departed, things could have gone wrong. Very wrong. The Brighton bubble could very easily have burst. The season – maybe even the Albion's status as a Premier League club – was teetering on a knife edge.

Brighton fans had two hopes to cling onto when waking up on September 10th, 2022, with their team managerless. The first were lessons from history; Potter was not the first boss to walk out mid-season on the Albion and he will not be the last.

It was a regular occurrence through the early 2000s. Micky Adams found the job of assistant manager to Dave Bassett at Leicester too good to turn down in October 2001. Peter Taylor replaced Adams and duly won the Division Two title seven months later.

Steve Coppell left the Albion in October 2003 for Reading, whose compensation offer proved very useful at a time when playing at Withdean was draining resources and there were public inquiries into a new stadium at Falmer to fund. No matter about Coppell's departure. Mark McGhee came in and Brighton ended the season promoted via the playoffs for the first and so far only time in their history.

The other source of hope was Tony Bloom. In 14 years at the helm, Bloom had appointed five managers. Gus Poyet, Oscar Garcia, Chris Hughton and Potter were all excellent appointments. The only black mark on Bloom's record was Sami Hyypia. Even so, an 80 percent strike rate is the sort of success most football club owners can only dream of.

Bloom's choice to become the sixth permanent boss of his tenure was Roberto De Zerbi, out of work since the war in Ukraine brought his time at the helm of Shakhtar Donetsk to a premature end. Both Bloom and deputy chairman Paul Barber deserve a huge amount of credit for the manner in which they identified De Zerbi and then went about acquiring his services.

The appointment was not without risk. Which is why it could have gone wrong. Very wrong. De Zerbi spoke little English when he took the job and his publicly stated ambition to be fluent by January seemed ambitious at best. Four months to master a new language? Good luck mate. De Zerbi of course was competent enough to give post-match interviews without relying on his translator within two.

Whilst Bloom undoubtedly got the appointment of De Zerbi right – make that an 83 percent success rate – it was the charismatic Italian who provided the magic to take Brighton to a level that only seemed possible in the sort of dream one has after too much super-strength cheddar.

Everything was stacked against De Zerbi when he arrived at the Amex. He had a group of players whose morale and confidence would have taken an understandable knock from seeing the entire coaching team they liked, respected and were into their fourth season working with walk out at the first sign of a big pay cheque.

De Zerbi's first task was lifting morale amongst players and fans. His infectious personality soon rubbed off on supporters; the way he celebrated each and every goal, the manner in which he talked about football with love and passion. Not since Poyet had a Brighton manager developed such a connection with the Albion faithful.

Then there was the profile of the squad. As already mentioned, it was one built for the way Potter played. Three at the back. Wing backs. Obsession with keeping possession. Taking the safe option to not give the ball away.

Compare that to De Zerbi's preferences. Throughout his managerial career, De Zerbi had always used a 4-2-3-1 formation. Risky passes in tight situations to draw the press of opponents. Once that had been achieved, lightning quick breaks sweeping from one end to the other.

It appeared at times as though Potter had a phobia of wingers; the sight of a Brighton player running past an opponent with pace and directness was rarer than a hen's teeth. De Zerbi depends on inverted wingers, charging up the pitch and cutting inside to cause havoc in opposition defences. His full backs are given the roles of creators as much as defenders.

On paper, the personnel did not appear there for De Zerbi to introduce his favoured formation and style of football. That was arguably the most significant challenge facing the new manager and one of the biggest risks in his appointment. The way he overcame it was incredible and is still yet to receive the credit it deserves.

De Zerbi was shrewd. He took the "If it ain't broke, don't fix it" approach for his first five games at the helm. Brighton had begun the season like a runaway train playing with a back three under Potter, so why rip it all up and start from scratch? If De Zerbi had swanned into the Amex, instantly changed everything and then failed to win any of his opening five matches, questions would have been asked and doubts put in many minds.

Instead, De Zerbi stuck with what had worked for Potter. Through five matches which he failed to win. That gave De Zerbi the worst start to a managerial reign of any Brighton boss in history. Proof, if ever it were needed, that one swallow does not make a summer. Martin Hinshelwood won his first game in charge, only to be sacked two months later. Jeff Wood was victorious on his debut in the dugout in a reign that lasted three months.

It was only one month into the job that De Zerbi switched to his 4-2-3-1 for the first time. The opponents? Chelsea. With a wonderful sense of timing, De Zerbi jettisoned what had worked for Potter in favour of his own style and approach on the day Potter returned to the Amex. A final score of Brighton 4-1 Chelsea tells you what an inspired decision that was.

With no opportunity to sign players to suit the way he wanted to play, De Zerbi instead had to find solutions from the squad bequeathed to him by Potter. This represents another example of the magic of the man. He coached different roles into existing players and in almost every case, the output of those individuals increased significantly.

Kaoru Mitoma made his full Premier League debut in the win over the Blues. There was no looking back from that point on for the man Tony accurately nicknamed The Japanese Bullet Train. Adam Lallana had been shunted around numerous midfield roles by Potter. De Zerbi in contrast settled on Lallana as a number 10 and only a number 10. His goal scoring record before a cruel season-ending injury in January spoke for itself.

De Zerbi's desire for creative full backs meant Pascal Gross being redeployed at right back for significant chunks of the campaign. Despite his newfound defensive duties, Gross contributed 10 goals and 10 assists. Numbers wise, it was the best season of his Albion career in both metrics.

Levi Colwill did not make his first Premier League start until November, just before the winter break for the World Cup. Having showcased his calmness on the ball and ability to play his way out of tight situations as demanded by De Zerbi, he was called up to the senior England squad within seven months.

De Zerbi had faith in Evan Ferguson to lead the line as the archetypal target man, the focal point of the attack. How many other managers would give an 18-year-old such responsibility? Having looked lightweight and with questionable decision making, Julio Enciso suddenly emerged as a number 10 with the potential to take English football by storm. De Zerbi has worked wonders with him.

It is Solly March, however, who remains the biggest example of De Zerbi's power. In 81 matches under Potter playing as a left wing back, right wing back, left winger, right winger, left back and any other position easily forgotten but tried, March contributed three goals and four assists.

De Zerbi decided that March's skills could be put to best use as an inverted right winger. The result was seven goals and seven assists in 27 matches before injury brought his season to a premature conclusion.

By not only overcoming all those challenges De Zerbi faced upon his September appointment but thriving in spite of them, he wrote his name into Albion folklore in the 2022-23 season. Sixth place. Europa League football. Two wins over Liverpool. Two wins over Chelsea. A point against treble winners Manchester City.

Six goals in a topflight game for the first time (sorry Potter, your five against Leicester was not in the history books for long). De Zerbi even became the first Brighton manager to taste victory away at Stoke City since 1961. It turned out the Albion under his leadership could do it on a cold Tuesday night in Stoke.

But what of a longer-lasting legacy for De Zerbi? That comes from the way in which he has changed the mindset of Brighton. No Albion fan will ever forget Hereford, two years at Gillingham, escaping relegation into League Two under Russell Slade on the final day of the season a mere 14 years before sixth place and European football was secured.

The days when everything Brighton achieved had to be put in the context of what Bill Archer, Greg Stanley and David Bellotti inflicted on the club and the fallout which lasted almost until the Amex opened in 2011 though are becoming numbered.

Potter tried to foster a mindset that Seagulls supporters should be grateful for each Premier League point he earned. It was born out in describing every opponent as fantastic, even if they were Norwich visiting for that 0-0 draw or a Burnley side without an away win all season. You know the one, when the Clarets went and hammered Brighton 3-0 at the Amex during that dismal spring run of 2022.

It also shone through in Potter's infamous history lesson comments. A couple of hundred Albion fans booing as Brighton extended their winless run (autumn 2021 rather than spring 2022) via a 0-0 draw at home to Leeds led Potter to say he needed a history lesson to understand why some were voicing their displeasure. The insinuation was clear – the Albion have spent only nine seasons in the top flight; be grateful for what you have, rather than dreaming of anything bigger.

No such attitude or illusions exist under De Zerbi. After eliminating Premier League leaders Arsenal from the League Cup, he called Brighton a big club. When the Albion were knocked out in the following round by League One Charlton Athletic, De Zerbi bristled for some time. Most managers would have responded to defeat against a club two divisions down the pyramid by dismissing the League Cup as unimportant. De Zerbi was livid that a potential route to silverware had disappeared.

One of the reasons the Albion went all the way to the FA Cup semi-finals was because of the fire lit under De Zerbi by that somewhat embarrassing evening at the Valley. He would not allow Middlesbrough, Stoke, Grimsby or even holders Liverpool to get in the way of Brighton stepping out at Wembley in the final four of the world's greatest cup competition.

Months before that April date under the arch against United, De Zerbi openly talked about European qualification being the aim for Brighton. In a matter of months, a club whose mindset had previously been survival was a success and anything else on top a bonus was completely transformed. We were no longer there just to make up the numbers.

De Zerbi believes the Albion should be challenging for the top six and reaching semi-finals and finals on a regular basis. Thar belief spread like wildfire to the players, as evidenced by the swagger and confidence that accompanied almost every performance from January onwards. It now extends to the terraces. And where it leads Brighton over the coming months and years – long after De Zerbi has departed for one of the biggest jobs in world football – will be fascinating.

The fact that the 2022-23 campaign could have gone wrong – very wrong – when Potter walked out for Chelsea is, for my money, what does indeed make it The Seagulls Best Ever Season. De Zerbi has worked magic to turn the Albion into a side the footballing world has ended up talking about, from Pep Guardiola to Jurgen Klopp to people down the pub. Even Victor Meldrew would be impressed.

WE ARE BRIGHTON.COM

Scott McCarthy
We Are Brighton. Com
Editor of Seagulls Best Ever Season - 2022-23

2022-22 Premier League Table

Pos	Team	Pld	W	D	L	GF	GA	GD	Pts
1	Manchester City	38	28	5	5	94	33	61	89
2	Arsenal	38	26	6	6	88	43	45	84
3	Manchester United	38	23	6	9	58	43	15	75
4	Newcastle United	38	19	14	5	68	33	35	71
5	Liverpool	39	19	10	9	75	47	28	67
6	Brighton	38	18	8	12	72	53	19	62
7	Aston Villa	38	18	7	13	51	46	5	61
8	Tottenham Hotspur	38	18	6	14	70	63	7	60
9	Brentford	38	15	14	9	58	46	12	59
10	Fulham	38	15	7	16	55	53	2	52
11	Crystal Palace	38	11	12	15	40	49	-9	45
12	Chelsea	38	11	11	16	38	47	-9	44
13	Wolves	38	11	8	19	31	58	-27	41
14	West Ham United	38	11	7	20	42	55	-13	40
15	Bournemouth	38	11	6	21	37	71	-34	39
16	Nottingham Forest	38	9	11	18	38	68	-30	38
17	Everton	38	8	12	18	34	57	-23	36
18	Leicester City	38	9	7	22	51	68	-17	34
19	Leeds United	38	7	10	21	48	78	-30	31
20	Southampton	38	6	7	25	36	73	-37	25

PREMIER LEAGUE RESULTS
2022-23

August
Manchester United 1 - 2 Brighton & Hove Albion
Brighton & Hove Albion 0 - 0 Newcastle United
West Ham United 0 - 2 Brighton & Hove Albion
Brighton & Hove Albion 1 - 0 Leeds United
Fulham 2 - 1 Brighton & Hove Albion

September
Brighton & Hove Albion 5 - 2 Leicester City

October
Liverpool 3 - 3 Brighton & Hove Albion
Brighton & Hove Albion 0 - 1 Tottenham Hotspur
Brighton & Hove Albion 0 - 2 Brentford
Brighton & Hove Albion 0 - 0 Nottingham Forest
Manchester City 3 - 1 Brighton & Hove Albion
Brighton & Hove Albion 4 - 1 Chelsea

November
Wolverhampton Wanderers 2 - 3 Brighton & Hove Albion
Brighton & Hove Albion 1 - 2 Aston Villa

December
Southampton 1 - 3 Brighton & Hove Albion
Brighton & Hove Albion 2 - 4 Arsenal

January
Everton 1 - 4 Brighton & Hove Albion
Brighton & Hove Albion 3 - 0 Liverpool
Leicester City 2 - 2 Brighton & Hove Albion

February
Brighton & Hove Albion 1 - 0 Bournemouth
Crystal Palace 1 - 1 Brighton & Hove Albion
Brighton & Hove Albion 0 - 1 Fulham

March
Brighton & Hove Albion 4 - 0 West Ham United
Leeds United 2 - 2 Brighton & Hove Albion
Brighton & Hove Albion 1 - 0 Crystal Palace

April
Brighton & Hove Albion 3 - 3 Brentford
Bournemouth 0 - 2 Brighton & Hove Albion
Tottenham Hotspur 2 - 1 Brighton & Hove Albion
Chelsea 1 - 2 Brighton & Hove Albion
Nottingham Forest 3 - 1 Brighton & Hove Albion
Brighton & Hove Albion 6 - 0 Wolverhampton Wanderers

May
Brighton & Hove Albion 1 - 0 Manchester United
Brighton & Hove Albion 1 - 5 Everton
Arsenal 0 - 3 Brighton & Hove Albion
Newcastle United 4 - 1 Brighton & Hove Albion
Brighton & Hove Albion 3 - 1 Southampton
Brighton & Hove Albion 1 - 1 Manchester City
Aston Villa 2 - 1 Brighton & Hove Albion

CARABAO CUP RESULTS
2022-23

Second Round
Forest Green Rovers 0 - 3 Brighton & Hove Albion

Third Round
Arsenal 1 - 3 Brighton & Hove Albion

Fourth Round
Charlton Athletic 0 - 0 Brighton & Hove Albion
Charlton won 4 - 3 on penalties

FA CUP RESULTS
2022-23

Third Round
Middlesbrough 1 - 5 Brighton & Hove Albion

Fourth Round
Brighton & Hove Albion 2 - 1 Liverpool

Fifth Round
Stoke City 0 - 1 Brighton & Hove Albion

Quarter-Final
Brighton & Hove Albion 5 - 0 Grimsby Town

Semi-Final
Brighton & Hove Albion 0 - 0 Manchester United
Manchester United won 7 - 6 on penalties

ACKNOWLEDGEMENTS

I WOULD LIKE to thank the following people for their help and support in trying to be able to make this second effort of publishing a second book on Brighton and Hove Albion Football Club, a reality. From last year's self-published version to this year's version, it has only been possible thanks to Mr Darren Gallis and Seagull Travel, who have sponsored the book. This has allowed me to work with a well-known publisher, Morgan Lawrence.

Thank you to everyone at Morgan Lawrence: Barrie Pierpoint, Lee Clark, Peter Andrews, Holly Mann, Harry Worgan, and Mathew Mann, who carefully guided me through the process of working with a book publisher and helped me understand how the process works.

A big thank you to my editor, Mr Scott McCarthy of We Are Brighton.com, who gave me the chance to write weekly on his website and to start to draw a following each week. His work and devotion to this project has been such a great help in the preparation of the text into a diarised book. Scott, from We Are Brighton.Com gave me my first chance of writing a weekly article and has religiously edited and taught me how to improve my writing style.

Also, a huge thank you to Mr Paul Camillin, Head of Media and Communications for his help in getting the material prepared for some of the text in this book.

Thank you to Paul Hazlewood, Brighton & Hove Albion club photographer, for providing us with some fantastic photos. Also, thanks to Rachel Thompson for allowing us to use the photo of Lewis Dunk.

Also, to Mr Johnny Cantor and Mr Warren Aspinall our faithful BBC Radio Sussex Sports Commentators, who provide for those supporters who cannot attend games and cannot afford to visit the away fixtures. A big thanks to them and also for allowing me to be a fly on the wall back on a very sunny afternoon at the Amex in October 2022, where I was able to see how it all works and how fascinating that was.

My dear wife of course as you can I am sure imagine, Kristine Susan Noble, who is a true Arsenal supporter as are her family, however the Albion is her second team now, and she occupies the seat next to me at every home game. I then relive the game two or three times to get the words on paper, and words are hard!

Finally, of course, my late mum, for letting me go to the Albion as a 10-year-old boy back in in 1966 and enjoy the games at the Goldstone Ground. (Dad was always busy playing football himself for Hove Grammar School Old Boys in Hove Park on a Saturday afternoon). However, I can still remember the smell of horse's liniment and my job when I was with him was to cut up the oranges for half time. Then it was all down to the local, many times it was the Grenadier at Hangleton where I would be stuck outside with a brown funny shaped bottle of Schweppes Ginger Beer and a packet of Smiths Ready Salted Crisps with the blue bag of salt inside, yummy! Those were days.

ABOUT THE AUTHOR

TONY NOBLE HAS been a Brighton & Hove Albion supporter since he attended his first game at the Goldstone Ground in 1966. After a couple of seasons spent watching from right at the front of the North Stand at the Goldstone, his family moved away from Hove to North Sussex when he was aged 12 years old, and Tony has been forced to watch from afar ever since until 2019.

Until the 2021-22 season that is. At the grand age of 66, Tony finally had his first-ever Brighton season ticket. Throughout the 2021 -2022 campaign, Tony shared his experiences of what it was like to attend Albion games regularly for the first time in more than half a century.

Tony has spent a big part of his life writing up legal documents and now finds great pleasure in writing about his boyhood passion, The Albion!

Tony responded to a social media advert for contributors for the famous website We Are Brighton.com. His submissions were accepted by the editor, and he started writing for every game in the 2021 -2022 season. He has continued this through the 2022-2023 season and feels that the tremendous efforts by the club, the staff as well as the coaching team and, of course, not forgetting all the players. So, to ensure a written record is preserved, a further second edition of the diarised book *Seagulls Best Ever Season* has been produced.